What English Really Is

A Self-Study Guide for Chinese Students on Mastering English

by

Ron Little

ISBN: 9798406738573

Dedication

For my loving parents, Libby and Anthony Little, my sister, Joanne,

and my extended family with everlasting gratitude.

Acknowledgments

Surely, whoever speaks to me in the right voice, him or her I shall

follow.

- Walt Whitman (1819-1892)

Many years ago, as a young teacher, I had the good fortune to encounter Dr. Caleb Gattegno (1911-1988) and his work on learning and teaching.   His teachings, based on a profound reverence for the individual and his/her innate ability to know, to learn bore a life-changing influence on my teaching as well as on my personal life. My debt to this great teacher is immeasurable.

Though the ideas presented herewith are inspired by the understanding he imparted to us, I make no claim that they would have his imprimatur.   They reflect my understanding of his insights into learning and teaching, coupled with my firsthand teaching experience. It is my sincere hope, however, that I have—in some way—done him justice.

I would also like to express my deep gratitude to Mira Erickson and Cecilia Bartoli.   It was Mira, the director of the World Trade Language Institute, who generously sent me to a week-long seminar at

Dr. Gattegno's school, Educational Solutions.   While there, it was Cecilia's loving understanding and teaching of Dr. Gattegno's work that opened my mind and, subsequently, paved the way.   Her seminar changed the path of my life.   I remain forever grateful to all three of them.

I would also like to extend my thanks to my colleague, Barbara J. Hoekje, who planted the idea of writing this book in my mind. Without Barbara's inspiration, this work would have never been born.

These acknowledgements would not be complete without giving due credit to the skills and generosity of IT technician, Hal Richman. Hal conscientiously attended to every aspect of formatting both the English version and the Chinese translation of this work for publication, while offering expert advice. I am forever grateful to him for his patience and kindness, his outstanding, dedicated work.

Contents

Dedication

Acknowledgments

Part I

For Chinese students everywhere—Misconceptions—Flat or round? —The right map—The purpose: a new view— Working directly on the language in the here and now—Why you tend to make the same mistakes—Not a direct translation—Inseparable partners: "how" and "what"—English is alive!—And, it's flexible!—All learning involves a "feel"—Integrated learning— A tutoring session—"Insights into Successful Learning" — American vs British English—Pace yourself, be patient with yourself—Allow me to explain—My story—"I know what it's like"—For teachers, too!—Our adventure.

Part II

Part III

Concept 1

Part IV

Concept 5

An English question, please—Chinese English question vs

English question—Wh-questions impacted—Mastery through

active practice—Answering questions: a round peg in a round

hole—Question and answer are related, connected, linked; they

are in harmony!—Major gears.

Phrasing a question for optimum learning— Questions are

golden opportunities for learning—Please speak up—

Client/lawyer; student/teacher.

The relationship between grammar and vocabulary—

Grammatical   structures or "You need a cup to hold your

tea"—The cup and the   tea—Beware: the counterproductive

practice of "getting only a general meaning"—The sentence

holds the key—The wrong approach vs the right approach—

Reminder: not the whole sentence!—The benefits—To your

advantage: English always tells the truth.

Concept 10

Part V

present—Pronunciation Point 4: Contractions—Two different
sounds—Pronunciation Passport—A word to the wise! (4)—
Oh, one last thing about pronunciation

Language is economical—Unintentionally misguided—
Awakening to the economy of language: a simple reflection—
An important insight: "chi"—How this applies to learning
English

Part VI

Remember: vocabulary is only part of the picture—Alert: 2
different things!—Using the dictionary—Dictionary and
Thesaurus—Cautionary Tale 2: Unreliable online sources—
Keep an eye out: nouns that can also be verbs!—Expressing the
whole noun—Quality vs Quantity— Again, pronunciation is
integral!—What a difference!: British vs American English—
Essential classroom vocabulary: Punctuation Marks and Parts of
Speech—Vocabulary for punctuation marks: it's all on your

All things are ready, if our minds be so.

—William Shakespeare

Part I

What It's About

For Chinese students everywhere

This book is especially for you, Chinese students of English, everywhere. Every topic, every discussion is tailored to your specific needs as native speakers of Chinese, learning English. It is a self-study guide aimed to help you master English by focusing on those areas where you tend to make the same mistakes. It is based on my firsthand experience working with Chinese students, both undergraduate and graduate, as a Faculty Writing Tutor/ESL Specialist in an American university.

In this one-on-one capacity, I have witnessed my Chinese students—though intelligent, dedicated and sincere—repeatedly make the same mistakes in speaking and writing English. Again and again, I have witnessed student after student with a substantial knowledge of English grammar and vocabulary, but with little understanding of how to use it correctly. Additionally, I saw that they had no exposure to

American English, its grammar, vocabulary or pronunciation.   Please forgive my frankness, but all their years of dedicated study—it seemed to me—did not serve them well in becoming successful speakers and writers of English.

Misconceptions

I came to realize that they had major misconceptions about English, which, unfortunately, caused them to be out of alignment with what English really is.   It was as if they were looking through the wrong end of a telescope, or walking west when they should be walking east.   I began to see that their exposure to English was predominantly passive.   That is to say, their study overemphasized memorizing grammar rules and vocabulary, while neglecting the essential, practical components of language learning: listening and speaking.   In this rigid mindset, everything—it seemed to me—was sacrificed for the sole purpose of passing standardized college entrance exams.

Consequently, their speaking, listening and writing skills were often lacking, leaving them at a serious disadvantage when attending

American colleges and universities, not to mention when participating

in daily life in an English-speaking country.

My experience has shown that there is an enormous gap

between what the average Chinese student "thinks" English is and

what, in fact, it really is.   Thus, this work is an attempt to narrow that

gap and ALIGN YOU, THE CHINESE STUDENT, TO WHAT

ENGLISH REALLY IS.

Flat or round?

As you know, people once believed that the earth was flat.

Consequently, much of what they perceived about life was based on

this false premise, an erroneous view that limited their understanding.

I think you would agree with me that they had the wrong concept of the

physical world we live in, that they were not aligned with the truth.

However, once they became aware, and changed their concepts of the

world, they were able to make, and have continued to make,

monumental discoveries.

So, I believe, is the case with many Chinese students learning

English.   Similarly, the Chinese student often has the wrong concept

of English, he tends to think that English is "flat," when, in fact, it's "round!"   This book, therefore, aims to help you change your concept of English, so that you, too, can make monumental discoveries, so that you may come to understand the truth about English, to acquire a sense of its spirit and, thereby, make greater progress.

The right map

I'm sure you would agree with me that having the wrong concept of English is akin to putting the wrong information in your GPS.   How can you arrive at your destination, i.e., master English, having put the wrong information in your GPS?   Thus, this book endeavors to help you put the right information into your "GPS device" so that you'll arrive at your destination without needless detours.   It's my hope that by giving you a more accurate map, you will become competent—and happy—speakers and writers of English.

The purpose: a new view

Your progress in English, dear student, depends, in large part, on becoming aware of your repeated mistakes and a sincere willingness to work on them.   My experience has shown that in spite of your good intentions in learning English, many of you remain unaware of the mistakes you repeatedly make.

Thus, the purpose of this work is:

1) to provide you with a new view on learning English, i.e., to give you a different lens through which to view your learning.

2) to help you become aware of your repeated mistakes in English and

3) upon identifying these mistakes, to focus on them—to learn from them—and thus align you with the correct understanding of English.   And, last, but not least,

4) to help free you from the constraints of rote learning, and thereby, help you to learn on your own, while in China as well as when studying, doing business and/or living in an English-speaking country.

In the following pages, we will carefully investigate and clarify—in simple language and with concrete examples—the concepts of English that Chinese students tend to misunderstand or ignore.   In short, we will provide you with a clearer, more accurate understanding of how American English is spoken and written in the 21st century.

Please keep in mind that every topic in this book is geared especially to your needs, whether you are an intermediate student, an advanced student, or a professional who uses English on a daily basis. Throughout, we aim to master English, not just to get by, not just for basic communication.   We always aim for mastery.

Working directly on the language in the *here and now*.

Throughout these pages, we will work directly on English as we encounter it in everyday situations, not through broad grammar rules which tend to distance you from what is happening in the moment. We will approach our study in a workmanlike manner, investigating what is before us in the "here and now", thereby, coming to a clearer understanding of what English is telling us in each situation.   This, in turn, will lead us to alignment and mastery.   Our examples will reflect casual, natural, everyday, native American-speaker English.

Why you tend to make the same mistakes

Please keep in mind that every language reflects a way of thinking that is revealed, largely, but not completely, in its grammatical structures.   As you will soon see, the concepts presented in this book focus on English patterns of thinking—English grammatical structures—that do not exist in Chinese.   As they do not exist in Chinese, what happens?   You tend to fall back on your Chinese grammatical structures when speaking and writing English.   In spite of your many years of studying English grammar, you are inclined to attach English words to Chinese grammar!   Result: the same mistakes again and again, causing poor communication between you and your native English-speaking counterparts.

This, of course, is "natural"—to a degree—but mastering English requires that you open your mind to a new—English—way of thinking.   In essence, English is asking you to change, to expand your awareness, to embrace a way of thinking that is outside your present understanding.   All true learning requires us to do so, be it English or anthropology.   And, fortunately, as humans, we have the ability to change, to learn!

Not a direct translation

A major component of our new view is: ONE LANGUAGE IS NOT A WORD-FOR-WORD TRANSLATION OF ANOTHER.   If this were the case, all you would have to do is memorize the dictionary to learn English.   But, this is not the case.   To do so would definitely be an erroneous approach, to have the wrong view.   Yet, how many students wrongly think this way?

All too often, we mistakenly assume that everyone, everywhere thinks as we do, constructs thoughts and sentences just as we do in our native language.   Nothing, dear student, could be further from the truth!   Therefore, it is important to always keep in mind that English is not a direct translation of Chinese, just as Chinese is not a direct translation of English.   Please keep in mind that each language reflects a way of thinking, a way of interpreting life.   This is an essential principle; its importance cannot be overemphasized.

Thus, acquainting yourself and being alert to the thinking and spirit of English is key to your success as a language learner.

It is my hope that in considering the ideas outlined in the following pages, you will change your approach to learning English. A new view—a new perception—will, in turn, have a positive impact on your learning.   It will help to free you.   You will "discover" a wider view.   You will be putting yourself on a path that will show you what English really is.   A change in your perspective will help to eliminate the many misconceptions that Chinese students tend to have about English; thereby, putting you in harmony with this new language, which, in turn will improve your proficiency, no matter what your level.   You will make greater strides.

Inseparable partners: "how" and "what"

          In keeping with this idea, it's imperative that you maintain an awareness—in all your learning—that "how" is as important as "what." What do I mean by this?   Students are unwittingly inclined to focus solely on "what" an individual word means, while neglecting to focus on "how" it is used in a sentence or question.   Similarly, they tend to focus on "what" a sentence or question means, while neglecting to focus on "how" the ideas in a sentence or question are expressed. Therefore, always keep in mind that "what" and "how" are inseparable; they belong together.   To separate them is to have a major misconception about learning English.   Be careful, then, that you don't foolishly "divorce" them.   If you "divorce" them, you will undermine your success in mastering English.   Be sure, then, that in all your learning that you always consider "how" as much as "what." THEY SHOULD ALWAYS BE CONSIDERED TOGETHER. Focusing solely on "what," while ignoring "how" will result in being stuck in Chinese English, or as my students lovingly call it,

"Chinglish."   As these pages unfold, you will see that a perception of

"how" is as important as "what."

English is *alive*!

It is also important to remember that language, be it English,

Chinese, Spanish, Dutch, etc., is *alive*!   It breathes, it moves, it flows.

In English—just as in Chinese—we laugh, we tell jokes, sing, discuss

the happenings of the day and open our hearts to those dearest to us.

All this, and much more is expressed in English!   Thus, language is

never static; IT'S FULL OF LIFE.

Unfortunately, classroom instruction—though well intended—

often presents English as if it had no life at all.   Consequently,

students often approach it in a mechanical way, as though it were a

mathematical formula.   Is it any wonder then that they are often

unable to express themselves freely in either speaking or writing?

English, like Chinese, is *alive!*   IT PULSES WITH LIFE!   Let us

take this understanding into account in all our learning, in our new

view.

And, it's flexible!

Because English is alive, it's flexible!   Regrettably, working principally from grammar rules tends to give you the misconception that English is inflexible, that it is stiff as a board, which it definitely is not.   Please keep in mind that English, like all other languages, is—by its very nature—flexible!   Language—by its very nature—has to be flexible!   It is my hope that the perspective offered in this book will help to free you from the confines of rigid rules and align you with everyday, living, breathing English.

All learning involves a "feel"

Since English is alive, it—like everything in life—has a "feel" to it.   This "feel" for English plays an important role in your learning and understanding.   I often find that students, in spite of their numerous years of studying English, lack a "feel" for it.   Therefore, aim to cultivate a "feel" for English in all your work.   Successful learning involves using your intuition; it's not just cut and dry facts. Please do not overlook this crucial component of your learning, of your new view.   Consider it often.   Consider it no matter the topic.

Integrated learning

It is important for us to keep in mind that mastering English requires constant, regular practice, not mindless repetitions, but—thoughtful—practice.   This involves integrating all your learning.   In other words, it's not a matter of having focused on one aspect of English yesterday, only to disregard it today, when focusing on another—new—aspect.   All true learning is linked, connected, integrated.   NO ASPECT OF LEARNING IS EVER ISOLATED; NO ASPECT OF LEARNING STANDS ALONE.

Allow me to give you an example of what I mean.   Let's say, for instance, that yesterday you studied how to use plurals in English and today you're learning how to use the past tense.   During the course of today's study, you say or write,

*I **bought** two new **shirt** online.*

Good, the verb tense from today's lesson is correct, but you overlooked the point of yesterday's lesson: plurals.   You should have said/written,

*I **bought** two new **shirts** online.*

This is linked, connected, integrated learning.   Although you were focusing on the past tense today, you did not lose sight of yesterday's focus: plurals.   You integrated yesterday's topic with

today's!   This is essential to your success in mastering English.

A tutoring session

This book parallels a tutoring session that you would have, if

you were to make an appointment with me in a university Writing

Center environment.   As in a tutoring session, we will pinpoint and

investigate the concepts of English that you tend to overlook or

misinterpret.   This will help you to gain mastery, a truer understanding

of what English really is, while eliminating confusion for you, your

listeners and readers.   This requires that you give each concept your

careful consideration—and practice—until it becomes second nature to

you.   Please keep in mind that though this book and your teachers can

help you, guide you, you, dear student, have to ultimately take

responsibility for your own learning.   No one can learn it for you.

"Insights into Successful Learning"

Woven into the fabric of this work are sections entitled,

"Insights into Successful Learning."   The insights given in these

sections are as important to your success in mastering English as are grammar, pronunciation, writing, etc. Please consider them as carefully as you would any English language topic. They will support you in all your learning. They will guide you in clearing the way to your success. They will fortify your new perspective.

American English vs British English

Throughout these pages, I stress America English. Why, you might rightfully ask? The majority of you will be attending American colleges and universities, communicating and interacting with Americans in your college, professional and social lives. Please keep in mind that British English differs CONSIDERABLY from American English in usage, vocabulary, pronunciation and, at times, spelling. It also differs considerably in demeanor! I have found that stressing British English—as is the current practice in China—widens the communication gap between you and your American professors, friends and colleagues, making it more difficult for you to understand and to be understood. Simply put, British English, though "lovely," impedes your progress as it's not, dear student, the language you will encounter when you reach American shores.

Whether in an American classroom or participating in everyday American life, the Chinese learner, with his British English perspective from China, will find himself out of alignment with his American counterparts.   It's as if they were not speaking the same language and, to a degree, they are not!   They are, as we say in everyday American English, NOT ON THE SAME PAGE!

It is my hope that the concepts presented in this book will help to put you in harmony with English as it is used in the U.S., particularly for those of you who plan to study in American colleges and universities, or to do business in this country.   Learning American English in today's world—it seems to me—is, at its essence, a very practical measure.   Kindly trust me in this!   I would ask that you heed the following remark by Irish playwright, Oscar Wilde (1854-1900):

We have really everything in common with America nowadays,

except, of course, language.

Witty and amusing, most certainly, but also very true!

Pace yourself, be patient with yourself

Please, do not be overwhelmed by the many concepts I have outlined for you in the following pages.   Take a workman's approach and pace yourself, working on one thing at a time.   Don't try to master all the concepts at once.   Take your time.   Be patient with yourself.   You decide upon the pace that best works for you, remembering that,

"Rome wasn't built in a day."

Allow me to explain

Throughout this book, I will be pointing out the mistakes that Chinese students tend to make in speaking and writing English. Please be assured that I am not ridiculing Chinese students nor the Chinese language or culture.

Our new perspective involves viewing language—whether Chinese or English—objectively, impartially, not suggesting in any way that one language is superior to the other.   In other words, you are being asked to observe how English behaves, just as a scientist would observe—neutrally—the behavior of the subject she is studying.   No judgment—or cultural bias—intended, just a simple, unprejudiced observation of how the English and Chinese languages behave.

So, when I say, "Chinese students," please understand that I am not berating Chinese students.   My purpose is to heighten your awareness, to facilitate your learning, to help you become better learners, better speakers and writers of English.

My story

Before closing this introduction, I would like to tell you something of my own story.   My interest in language began when I was a boy.   I was fascinated by my Italian grandparents and American parents who communicated with each other in Italian.   (As is often the case among immigrant families in the US, the mother tongue is sadly lost by the second generation.   The language is lost, but not the culture!)

My young mind could not fathom how they could possibly understand each other.   To my young ear, Italian sounded a jumble, a muddle, a mishmash.   (To this day, I can still see my sister and me in my grandparents' home, watching, listening, our heads turning from grandparents to parents and parents to grandparents as they conversed in Italian).

By high school, this fascination with language evolved into a deep admiration for people who spoke more than one language.   I was in awe of them and longed—in my impressionable, enthusiastic adolescence—to be like them, to possess this quality of existing in, at least, two different worlds.   This interest led me to major in Spanish in college.   My desire to master Spanish, in turn, expanded into studying and working in both Spain and Latin America.

"I know what it's like"

I mention these experiences to assure you, dear student, that I am well aware of the challenges that you face when learning a second language, particularly while living in a foreign culture.   I've had first-hand experience of the joys—and frustrations—of attempting to understand and to be understood, of attempting to produce new, different sounds.   I know how it feels to be on the outside of a culture, looking in and longing to enter.   I know how it feels to be uncertain, to wonder if I was expressing myself correctly, clearly.   I point this out to verify that I have walked the same path as you, that I can easily empathize with the challenges you encounter in learning English and using it in an English-speaking country.   As these pages unfold, please know that I am speaking from first-hand experience, that I am walking by your side.

For teachers, too!

One last point: It is also my hope that this book will be of service to Chinese teachers of English in China as well as English teachers everywhere to better understand—and guide—their Chinese students to success.   It is hoped that they will be encouraged to integrate the ideas and concepts in this book into their understanding and daily lessons.

Our adventure

Okay, dear student, let's roll up our sleeves and get started. We are about to embark on a wonderful—and I trust insightful and worthwhile—adventure together.   I sincerely hope that you will enjoy it and that you will gain a clearer, truer understanding of what English really is.

Part II

First Things First

The real "problem"

Students erroneously tend to think their main "problem" is vocabulary. I understand this viewpoint—it seems logical—but I can assure you, dear student, that vocabulary is not your primary "problem." Your "problem" is understanding and using the fundamental grammatical structures of English correctly. If you don't have a grasp of these structures, you will end up, as we have pointed out, attaching English words to your native Chinese grammar. Result: retarded progress and poor communication skills. In other words, native English speakers will have difficulty in understanding you.

A false premise

I strongly feel that over-stressing vocabulary is fundamentally a false premise, a major misconception about learning English. Why, you may well ask? Because vocabulary doesn't provides you with a foundation on which to build, on which to grow. (If vocabulary, were all-important, students would only have to memorize the dictionary to speak English.   But this, of course, is not true!).   Chinese students, more than anything else, need to master the fundamental grammatical structures of English, structures that DO NOT EXIST IN CHINESE, BUT ARE CRUCIAL TO ACCURATE COMMUNICATION IN ENGLISH.

So, as we have previously pointed out, please keep in mind that learning a new language is not solely a matter of "what" something means (vocabulary); it's equally a matter of "how" it's expressed (structures).   Always keep in mind that,

1) "how" is as important as "what" and that

2) grammatical structures always teach you "how;" they will always align you with correct English.

This is an essential principle.   It's crucial to mastering English.   So, please don't lose sight of it!   Keep it always at the fore of your mind.

The foundation

For you, dear Chinese student, the following four concepts of English—which I call "The 4 Golden Keys to English"—form the very foundation to your mastery of English.   They will open the door to aligning you to a correct understanding of English.   (Remember this book is geared specifically to the particular needs of the Chinese student).   These "keys" are essential to your success in spoken as well as written English.   Absolutely essential!   They are crucial!

Like the foundation and studs of a house, "The 4 Golden Keys to English" keep English standing up straight; they keep it erect.   They form the essential structure on which English——for the Chinese learner——is based.   Without them, English collapses; it falls apart. Without them, Chinese students fail to make themselves clearly understood, thereby, coming across as poor speakers and writers of English, while confusing their English-speaking listeners and readers.

"Blind spot"

Sadly, I have found that the majority of Chinese students— again, I ask your pardon for my candor—tend to ignore these concepts when speaking and writing English.   Why do they do this?   The answer is quite simple.   As we have indicated above, these four foundational concepts—"The 4 Golden Keys to English"—do not exist in the Chinese language.   Consequently, Chinese students are inclined not to "see" them in English.   As they tend not to "see" them, they tend not use them.   Thus, I also call these four foundational major concepts of English "blind spots" for the Chinese student.

Please understand that this is not a value judgment, nor a permanent condition.   ALL OF US ARE PRONE TO "SEE" WHAT WE ALREADY KNOW.   It's a human trait that has nothing to do with nationality!   "The 4 Golden Keys to English" which you are about to encounter are, in essence, an attempt to help you "see" what you normally don't see.   (This is likewise true for all the other "Concepts" in this book.   Please notice that they are called "Concepts," not "Chapters."   We have done this to emphasize that these "concepts"—which do not exist in Chinese—are vital to English, that they play a major role in English.   As such, they warrant your careful attention).   May I add, dear student, that your success in mastering English depends on your seeing them, understanding them and using them?   They are an integral part of English.

Not a permanent condition

As previously noted, "blind spots," are not, in any way, a permanent condition.   (Please remember that, as human beings, we have the ability to change.   Please remember that learning is essentially about change!) I am implying, however, that you cannot be too diligent in focusing your attention on these "blind spots" until you "see" them, that you cannot be too diligent in focusing your attention on them until they become second nature to you, no matter your level of proficiency. (Please believe me when I say that advanced-level students as well as PhD candidates and working professionals have the same challenges with these concepts as do beginning and intermediate students).

By diligently putting your attention on these concepts—this essential foundation—you will not only eliminate the "blind spots," but you will simultaneously put yourself in alignment with what English really is. Like a surfer, you will be riding the wave; you'll be one with English!

A neutral perspective

Please allow me to reiterate that I use the term "blind spots" from a purely neutral perspective.   Again, the scientist impartially observing behaviors.   I am not, in any way, belittling Chinese students or the Chinese language.   I am simply juxtaposing the two languages so as to create—through contrast—understanding and clarity for you.

As stated previously, my purpose it to help you identify your major

weaknesses so that you can focus on them, learn from them, and

thereby become successful speakers and writers of English.

Part III

The 4 Golden Keys to English

Mastering English for the Chinese student involves the following four major—**vital**—concepts of English.   Again, for the Chinese student, these concepts are the very foundation for success in English!

> Concept 1:   Golden Key 1 Plurals
>
> Concept 2:   Golden Key 2 "a"
>
> Concept 3:   Golden Key 3 "the"
>
> Concept 4:   Golden Key 4 Tense

As native speakers of Chinese, this simple knowledge—these *4 Golden Keys*—is invaluable to you! We cannot over-stress their importance to your proficiency in English.   They are THE MOST IMPORTANT GRAMMATICAL CONCEPTS for Chinese students. Please remember that accurate communication depends on them. Without them, you will be misunderstood, causing confusion for native speakers of English.   Additionally, you will unwittingly entangle yourself in numerous other grammatical errors.   Please believe me, this is not an exaggeration.   "The 4 Golden Keys to English"—for the

Chinese student—are critical for your ultimate competence in English. If I could write this paragraph, dear student, in multi-colored, flashing neon lights, I would do so!   That's how important "The 4 Golden Keys to English" are to your success in spoken and written English.

Yes, I know that you are familiar with these words and, perhaps, the rules regarding them.   In fact, you might be thinking to yourself as you read this, "You're kidding us, Professor Little.   We've known this since day 1."   Yes, dear student, you're absolutely right, but here's the rub.   You are familiar with these words, BUT FAIL TO RECOGNIZE THEIR VITAL IMPORTANCE.   As a result, you neglect to use—to integrate—them in your speaking and writing.   In other words, you tend not to see their importance for clear and accurate communication in English.   Consequently, you leave your native speaker of English confused, uncertain as to your meaning.

Mastering these four concepts will align you with the spirit of English; they will help you immensely in acquiring a "feel" for English.   Your challenge then, dear student, is TO OPEN YOUR MIND to a new—different—way of perceiving.   Your challenge is to EXPAND YOUR WAY OF THINKING until these concepts, "The 4 Golden Keys," make sense to you, until they become second nature to you.   And they will, if you make the effort.   Speaking English without them is like attempting to solve a math problem without, let's say, the numbers 2, 5, 7 and 8.   How will you ever arrive at the correct answer without using these crucial numbers?   Allow me to assure you that by concentrating on "The 4 Golden Keys," you will be unlocking the door to English and your ultimate accomplishment.

Concept 1

Golden Key #1: Plurals *(Which word expresses how many?)*

Noun or adjective?

Obviously, both the East and the West have the concept of plural.   (We all want to know how much it costs, how far it is, how many there are, how much money we have, etc.) The issue of plurals in English vs Chinese boils down to this simple awareness: WHICH WORD IN A SENTENCE—OR A QUESTION—EXPRESSES THE PLURAL?   This simple question is of the utmost importance to you. Let's investigate what I mean.

In Chinese, the adjective (*many, several, a few, some, 6*, etc.) alone expresses the plural, not the noun!   The adjective in Chinese is the crucial word; it's the word that determines "how many," "how much."   In other words, THE CHINESE ADJECTIVE IS THE POWER WORD in signaling the plural.   Consequently, the Chinese noun remains unchanged, whether singular or plural in meaning.

In English, however, it's the opposite: the noun—not the adjective—expresses "how many," "how much" and it changes.   The noun in English—as regards plurals—is the crucial word, the word that determines the plural and thus communicates the correct meaning.   In other words, THE ENGLISH NOUN IS THE POWER WORD in signaling plural.

To facilitate your understanding, let's take a closer look at this, i.e., let's investigate the concept by using concrete examples so that you can see how it works in Chinese and in English.   (When I say, "Chinese says," I'm translating the Chinese concept/sentence into English words).

Chinese says:

*He has **many** friend.*

Notice that the adjective, **many,** carries the meaning of plural, not the noun, **friend.**   The noun, **friend,** remains unchanged.

English, on the other hand, says:

*He has many **friends.***

Notice that the noun, **friend,** adds "s" to signal plural, thereby agreeing with the adjective **many.**

This is the whole matter in a nutshell!   IN CHINESE, THE ADJECTIVE—ALONE—EXPRESSES PLURAL, WHILE THE NOUN REMAINS THE SAME.   IN ENGLISH, HOWEVER, THE NOUN EXPRESSES THE PLURAL AND CHANGES TO AGREE

WITH THE ADJECTIVE.   This is an essential concept for you to understand, dear student, if you want to speak and write English correctly, if you want to be clearly understood.

How it manifests in your English

Sadly, my experience has shown that the majority of Chinese learners—advanced students as well as beginner and intermediate students, not to mention working professionals—are inclined to disregard this all-important, fundamental feature of English in both speaking and writing!   Despite its simplicity, despite its presence in all of English—in both spoken and written English—it, invariably, escapes your attention.   That's why I call it a "blind spot!"

Again and again, I hear and see, "five house," "many bicycle," "some cup,"   "several idea," "ten dollar," etc.   How could this be I ask myself?   How could it be that Chinese students, renowned for their intelligence in learning and understanding the intricacies of advanced math and science, repeatedly neglect to make this minor adjustment to their awareness?   In fact, I would venture to say, dear reader, that if I had a dollar for every time one of my Chinese students omitted a plural noun (i.e., a final "-s" in either spoken or written

English), I'd be one of the richest men in the world!   Again, please

believe me, I do not exaggerate.

I beg you to take a few moments to reflect on this all-important

grammatical feature of English.   It's so simple, so close to us as to

escape our awareness.   Yet, so very much depends upon it in being

correctly understood, so much depends upon it in mastering English.

To help you better understand, let's take a look at a few more

examples.   (Again, when I write "Chinese says," I'm translating the

Chinese concept/sentence into English words).

Chinese says,

My uncle has two car.   (the adjective **two**—alone—indicates

plural, not the noun, **car**).

English, however, says,

My uncle has two cars.   (the noun **cars**—principally—

indicates plural and agrees with **two**).

Chinese says,

He broke some plate.   (the adjective **some**—alone—indicates

plural, not the noun, **plate**).

English, however, says,

*He broke some **plates**.*   (the noun **plates**—principally—

indicates plural and agrees with **some**).

Chinese says,

*They have several **reason** for their decision.*   (the adjective

several— alone—indicates plural, not the noun, **reason**).

English, on the other hand, says,

*They have several **reasons** for their decision.*   (the noun

reasons—principally—indicates plural and agrees with **several**).

Allow this concept and the above examples to penetrate

your mind, your understanding.   In doing so, you will better

understand the importance of changing your perception when learning a

new language!   Again, THIS UNDERSTANDING OF HOW

ENGLISH EXPRESSES THE PLURAL IS PIVOTAL TO YOUR

SUCCESS IN SPEAKING AND WRITING ENGLISH.   I say pivotal

because plurals impact other important aspects of English grammar,

pivotal because plurals support other aspects of English.   Like the

concrete foundation and the wooden studs in a house, they keep

English standing up straight, strong!

How it sounds to a native English speaker

Allow me to show you how this Chinese English "sounds" to the native speaker of English.   Let's say, for example, a Chinese student says or writes, "I have many friend."

This sentence not only sounds "weird" to the English ear, it doesn't, in fact, make sense!   It's like pointing up and saying "down." The Chinese English sentence—to the English ear—is contradictory, confusing, illogical!   Please bear with me as I attempt to convey to you what transpires in the mind of a native English speaker.

When a native speaker of English hears **"many"**—as in the above example—she expects to hear—or to read—**"friends**, " but the Chinese speaker says, **"friend."**   What's going on?   How can this be?   To the English ear and mind, it's a contradiction!   It doesn't add up!   To make sense in English, it has to be *"many* **friends**," plain and simple!   (Of course, we understand the Chinese speaker's meaning, but it tends to be misleading and confusing, causing the native English speaker to pause and consider what the Chinese speaker actually means, "Oh, yes, I see, he means, 'I have many friends.' " Of equal importance, this repeated incorrect English does not reflect your intelligence.   It gives the impression that you don't speak, write or understand English well).   Though it may seem like a small thing to you, dear student, to English, it's A BIG THING!

Using ourselves differently

Using plurals correctly also requires a different use of your physical energy.   It requires you to use more of yourself—of your body—in your learning, not just your ability to memorize data.   It requires that you use your breath differently.   It requires you to enunciate an [s], [z] or [əz] sound at the end of a noun when speaking—a pronunciation new to you—as well as the addition of an [s] or [es] when writing.   I can assure you that diligently practicing this pronunciation will, without a doubt, put you in alignment with correct English.   It will open doors to clear, correct communication!

I can well understand that articulating an [s], [z], or [əz] at the end of a word may seem "unnatural" to you.   After all, you do not have this pronunciation at the end of words in Chinese; you are not used to it.   But, dear student, it's not "unnatural" to the native English speaker!   It's an integral part of the English language.   This new, different use of your energy in speaking English is as important to you as its grammar and vocabulary.   I reiterate, IT'S AS IMPORTANT AS ITS GRAMMAR AND VOCABULARY.

If you feel that this new pronunciation is difficult, I would encourage you to see it as "different," not as "difficult."   That is to say, it's not really "difficult;" it's "only different."   If it were difficult, native speakers of English would not be able to do it, but we all do! Kindly consider the following.

Strengthening your understanding of plurals

As you now know that plurals are a crucial feature of English, try to seek every opportunity to heighten your awareness of them. When reading, for example, pay close attention to the plurals.   DON'T SKIM OVER THEM AS IF THEY DIDN'T EXIST.   In fact, I would strongly recommend that you take a pen or highlighter and mark every plural you encounter in your reading.   You will be amazed to discover how many times they occur.   Of equal importance, I would highly recommend that your pronounce these words as you highlight them, making sure that you actually are pronouncing the final sound.   TAKE SPECIAL CARE IN LISTENING TO YOURSELF.

I mention this careful self-listening because I have found that students often "think" they are pronouncing the final ([s], [z] or [əz]) sound, when actually they are not!   (They "hear" it in their mind, but are not articulating it in their mouth).   This, therefore, might be an excellent exercise to practice with a friend.   In this way, you can check each other carefully to be sure you are articulating the sounds.

In addition, when listening to native speakers of English, whether in conversation or on TV or in a movie, listen carefully for the plural sound.   Soon, you will find yourself saying, "Ah, yes, they said, 'All the houses on our street are covered in snow.' "

West and East

As we have discussed, every culture has a different way of interpreting life.   One is not superior to another; they're just different. We in the West, just as you in the East, look at the world around us and see that there is more than one tree, more than one house, more than one car, etc.   We in the West express this perception by stressing the noun and saying, "trees," "houses," "cars," etc.   (Allow me to point out to you that the noun changes form in all European languages to express plural, be it French, Spanish, German, etc.) In the East, you, too, perceive plural, but to express it you stress the adjective, leaving the noun unchanged. The beauty of learning a new language is that it opens our minds to seeing the world—life itself—from a different perspective. It helps us to realize that not everyone in the world views life as we do. This, in turn, helps us become better, more understanding human beings! This is true education; this is true learning.

Insights into Successful Learning 1

Attitude is everything!

We cannot overemphasize the importance of a positive attitude in learning.   It plays a vital role in learning English as it does in every aspect of life.   Your attitude toward mastering English will determine your success or your failure.   If you have a positive attitude, an "I-can-do-it" attitude; if, in other words, you are interested, you will make great progress.   However, if you don't have a positive attitude, if you are not interested, then, there is little anyone or anything can do for you.   If you view English as something unattainable, something difficult, something forced on you to learn, then, of course, you will probably not succeed.

Beware of considering English as something very "foreign," something beyond your reach, because it isn't.   To think so, dear student, is to defeat yourself.   As humans, we have much more in common than we have differences.   Whether we are Chinese, Americans, Spaniards, French, etc., we all want the best for ourselves and our loved ones, we all want to prosper, to be happy, healthy, to have friends, to enjoy life fully.   If you stop to reflect on this, you will

soon discover that what we share as humans far outweighs our
(cultural) differences.   Reflecting on this, you may soon discover that
English is not so "foreign" after all!

Keep in mind that we all learned our native language.   If we
have learned our native language, we can learn another language.   The
ability is in all of us.   You can do it.   Just be sure you keep a
positive, open attitude.   If you don't have a positive attitude, if you are
not interested, you will be undermining all your efforts.   Remember
that you are the only one who can provide the interest.   An attitude of
interest is fundamental to your learning and ultimate success!

Interest is the soil in which intelligence and knowledge grow.

—Author unknown

Investigations and discoveries

As our journey unfolds, may I suggest that you aim to create
"an attitude of investigation" in all your study, whether working alone,
with friends or in class?   Having "an attitude of investigation"—I
feel—is an essential component of successful learning.   It means
being alert, watching, being awake to what is happening in the "here
and now."   It's the opposite of memorizing.

Attempt, then, to maintain an attitude of: "Let's see what I'll discover today."   The process of learning is a process of making discoveries.   Cultivate an attitude of:

"Let's take a closer look and determine what the sentence/question is telling us."

"What do I need to pay extra special attention to?"

Approaching your learning as investigation—no matter what the topic—you will soon come to realize an important insight: investigations always lead to discoveries.   The two go hand-in-hand. Columbus investigated the shape of the earth and discovered a new continent.   Copernicus investigated the heavens and discover that the sun, not the Earth, was the center of our solar system!   And, in a way, the same principle holds true for you in your learning English. Always approach your learning in the spirit of investigation and you're bound to discover something of importance.   In the process of making investigations and discoveries, you will begin to acquire—as we have discussed before—a "feel" for English.   You will be aligning yourself with English.   You will be acquainting yourself with what English really is.   Most important, you will begin cultivating your intuition.

Expanding our way of thinking

In any learning process, we encounter ideas/concepts that are new to us, that are outside our present understanding and experience. Whenever this occurs, we have to expand our way of thinking—to open ourselves—and integrate these new ideas/concepts into our understanding.

For example, when you first encounter the English word "table," you have no difficulty in understanding it because the idea/the concept of "table" exists in Chinese; the concept of "table" already exists in you.   Easy!

However, when you encounter the English concept of plurals ("tables"), which is a new concept for you—a concept which doesn't exist in Chinese—you have to open your mind to a new perspective, a different way of thinking and of physically using yourself.   You have to go beyond your present understanding to integrate this new concept—this new idea—into your present understanding.   As we have mentioned before, this is at the heart of all learning, be it English or math.   Each of the concepts that you encounter in this book require that you expand your present way of thinking.   This you can do, if you put your mind to it, i.e., if you are willing and make the effort.

As we have discussed, Chinese students tend to repeatedly make the same mistakes in English.   Why?   Because essentially they have not expanded their way of thinking; they have not extended themselves beyond their Chinese world.   Please understand that I'm not suggesting, in any way, that Chinese students are poor learners. All nationalities tend to have this same characteristic, i.e., we all tend to cling to what we already know, never considering that there may be different ways to express our thoughts and feelings. It's a universal human experience.   I point this out to stress to you that mastering English requires that you open your mind to a different way of thinking.   It is not just a matter of learning English words and attaching them to your native Chinese grammar.

The concepts presented in this work are designed to help you effortlessly expand your thinking, to help you open your mind to a new, different view.   The process is neither difficult nor painful.   It simply requires a willingness to be open, to go beyond your present understanding.

Concept 2

Golden Key 2: "a" *(A small word with B-I-G meaning)*

"a" means 1, the opposite of "many"

Now that you have an understanding of the concept of plurals—and their importance—in English, it's just a short step away to understanding "a." Basically, "a" means "one." (We might put it this way: "a"=1). In essence, "a" makes a distinction between many/several things (plurals) and just one thing. So, if you are speaking of only one thing, English requires that you express that one thing/that singular noun with the word "a." THIS IS A FUNDAMENTAL PRINCIPLE OF ENGLISH: it's nothing more complex than that.

Therefore, the majority of singular—countable—English nouns will never stand alone as they do in Chinese; they will usually be expressed by saying "a." In other words, don't think "smart-phone," —as you do in Chinese—think "a smart-phone." Don't think "computer,"—as you do in Chinese—think "a computer." Don't think "car,"—as you do in Chinese—think "a car." Let's investigate!

An insightful scenario

Please give the following scenario your careful consideration as I'm sure it will help you to better understand the use and importance of "a." It will provide you with important insights into speaking and writing English correctly. Here we go.

If you show a Chinese student a pencil and ask him, "What's this?", chances are, he will say, *"pencil."* I'm sorry, dear student, but that's not correct English! That's Chinese English; it's an English word attached to Chinese grammar and readily reveals a student out of alignment with English. Now, ask the same question to a native speaker of English and he will spontaneously say, *"a pencil."* Now, that's English; it's in alignment with itself.

Here's another example to help you understand: Ask a Chinese student, *"What do you have in your hand?"* and, chances are, she will say, "pen." Again, I apologize, but that's not correct English! That, once again is Chinese English; it's an English word attached to Chinese grammar. Again, it readily reveals a student out of alignment with English. Ask the same question to a native speaker of English and she will spontaneously say, *"a pen."* Allow me to point out that the

answer *"pencil,"* "pen" may sound "right" to you, but to English, it
sounds "wrong," because it is!

Please understand that I'm not nitpicking.   This seemingly
minor difference between English and Chinese is of the utmost
significance to you in being understood correctly!   As with plurals, so
much accurate communication depends upon it.   As we've pointed
out, if you fail to use plurals, English collapses.   The same holds true
for "a."   Failure to use "a" and, again, English collapses.

(Please note that as with plurals, the concept of "a" is an
essential principle in English and in all Western languages.   You'll
find it in French, Spanish, German, Greek, etc.).

And, allow me to point out to you once again that although "a"
is a small word and may appear insignificant to you, that a final "-s"
sound at the end of a word may likewise appear insignificant, they are
not—by any means—insignificant in English.   THEY'RE BIG
BUSINESS!   Please take heed!

Invaluable practice

Now let's put this basic English concept into practical use.
Look around you now and begin to name what you see.   If, for

example, you are in the library studying, you might look around and say: *"a chair," "a table," "a student," "a laptop," "a pen,"* etc.   (I highly recommend that you make a written list as you do this).   If you are at home studying in your room, you might look around and say: *"a desk," "a lamp," "a bed," "a rug," "a picture",* etc.   Write these items down.

Try the same exercise while walking down the street: *"a tree," "a store," "a girl," "a boy," "a dog," "a bus," "a restaurant," "a taxi," "a house,"* etc.   Write these items down.   Again, the simple, neutral state of a singular—countable—English noun will almost always be expressed by using that little, but all-important, word "a," which, in essence, simply means "one."   Whatever singular object/thing you perceive in English will—almost always—be accompanied by "a." Think of it like this: *"What's that?" "a teapot."   "What's that?" "a book."   "What's that?" "a bowl of rice."*

Don't stop there!

I would encourage you to practice this simple exercise regularly, without paper and pencil, no matter where you are, no matter what you're doing.   Make a point of silently naming to yourself the—

singular—objects that you see in your daily life: "a sweater," "a cafe," "a spoon," "a traffic light," "a flag," "a crosswalk," "an elevator," "a magazine," "a picture," etc.

This is worthwhile practice that will help you master English, that will help put you in touch with—real, living—English, not with stiff, rote-learned grammar rules. In essence, this regular practice will help harmonize you to what English really is! Please trust me in this! This concept of "a" is completely new to you. It doesn't exist in Chinese. Therefore, it will require constant practice. Practice in this way until it becomes second nature to you, no matter where you are, no matter what you're doing.

Take it a step further

I would also highly recommend that you take this exercise one step further by making a simple sentence or question from the list of the objects you've made. You might write, for example:

> *There's **a lamp** on my desk.*
>
> *She's looking for **a stapler.***
>
> *I would love to have **a car** like that!*
>
> *Does your cousin have **a bike**?*

*Do they live in **a house** or **an apartment**?*

(In such exercises, please don't feel that you have to make long, complex sentences.   It's not necessary.   A simple sentence that expresses your idea is all that is required.   This is both natural and spontaneous; it is, in essence, using language as native speakers do!).

Pronunciation of "a"

One last thing before closing this discussion: the word "a" is pronounced differently from the letter "A."   The word is pronounced /ə/; the letter /**ei**/.   Therefore, English says /ə/ movie, not /**ei**/ movie.

Attention!

Please keep in mind that if a noun begins with a vowel (*a, e, i, o, u*), "a" becomes "an," as in "an **a**pple," "an **e**lephant," "an **i**dea," "an **o**nion," "an **u**mbrella."

Concept 3

Golden Key 3: "the" *(Another small word with B-I-G meaning)*

Establishing another contrast

Now that you have a clearer understanding of how English expresses the difference between many things (plurals) and one thing ("a/an"), it will be easier to understand the idea of "the." Let's investigate!

If you are referring to A SPECIFIC THING, TO A SPECIFIC OBJECT, English says "the." Here are a few examples to clarify this point.

Example 1:

The laptop *I want to buy is expensive.*

In this situation, we are referring to a SPECIFIC "laptop." Which laptop? *"the laptop* **I want to buy**." Therefore, English says *"***the** laptop" (*"the"* answers the question *"*Which laptop?" "Which one?"* "The laptop [the one] **I want to buy**.").

Now, contrast this with,

*I want to buy **a laptop.***

In this case, it's NOT A SPECIFIC *"laptop"* that you want to buy.   It's just "a/one/any" laptop.   Therefore, English says, *"**a** laptop."*

Ponder this English perception until it makes sense to you.   If you give it your careful consideration, based on this example, it will become clear.   Please remember that the more you consider this concept in all your investigations into English, the clearer it will become to you.

Example 2:

> ***The*** *house they rented is over 200 years old.*

As in the previous example, we are referring to a PARTICULAR, a SPECIFIC thing.   In this sentence, a PARTICULAR "house."   Which house?   Which "house" are you talking about?   Which "house" are you referring to*?*   *"the house **they rented."***   Therefore, English says *"**the** house."*   (Again, *"the"* answers the question *"Which house?"* "Which one?"   *"The house[the one]* **they rented."**)

Contrast this idea with,

> *They rented **a house.***

In this case, it's NOT A PARTICULAR "house" they rented. It's simply "a/one/any" "house."   Therefore, English says, "a house."

Again, I ask you to ponder this English perception as expressed in this example until it makes sense to you.   If you give it careful thought—and practice—it will reveal itself to you.   Remember the more you consider it, the clearer it will become to you!

Now, consider this.

Example 3:

*He dropped **a cup**.*

vs

*He dropped **the cup**.*

In the first sentence, English says "**a** cup" because it's not a specific cup that we're talking about; it's just ANY cup, no SPECIFIC cup at all.   Thus, "**a** cup."

In the second sentence, English says "**the** cup" because the speaker(s) is referring to, the speaker(s) is talking about a DEFINITE, a SPECIFIC "cup," "the cup" they had been discussing in their conversation.   Thus, "**the** cup."

Again, dear student, please ponder this English perception until it becomes clear to you.   As this concept doesn't exist in your native

Chinese, it will require a concerted effort on your part to make it your

own!   Please be assured that it will come; it will reveal itself to you!

Practice with "the"

Now that you have an understanding, we might say an "entry"

into the concept of *"the"*—no matter how slight—take out the list of

words that you wrote in the library, in your room at home while

studying, while walking down the street, etc.   Next, change, for

example, "**a** chair" to "**the** chair," "**a** bed" to "**the** bed," "**a** restaurant"

to "**the** restaurant" and write a sentence or question with your word of

choice.

You might write sentences such as:

Example 1:

> ***The chair*** *in my room is red.*

(Notice that you're referring to a PARTICULAR chair.   Which

chair?/Which one?   "the chair **in my room**").

The concept of "the" applies to plural nouns as well:

> ***The chairs*** *in my room **are** red.*

(Notice, again, that you're referring to a PARTICULAR chairs.

Which chairs?/Which ones?   "the chairs **in my room.**"   Notice how the plural impacts the verb; "is" becomes "are").

Example 2:

*We always go to **the restaurant** near campus.*

(Notice that you're talking about a SPECIFIC restaurant.   Which

restaurant?/Which one?   "the restaurant **near campus**").

Again, the concept of "the" applies to plural nouns as well:

*We always go to **the restaurants** near campus.*

(Notice, again, that you're referring to a PARTICULAR restaurants.

Which restaurants?/Which ones? "the restaurants **near campus**").

Example 3:

*She wrote **the novel** two years ago.*

(Notice that you're talking about *a* PARTICULAR novel.   Which

novel?/"Which one?"   "the novel **she wrote two years ago**").

Again, this concept applies to plural nouns as well:

*She wrote **the novels** two years ago.*

(Notice that you're talking about SPECIFIC novels.   Which

novels?/Which ones?   "the novels **she wrote two years ago**").

Example 4:

***The sign** is in Chinese and English.*

(Notice that you're talking about a SPECIFIC sign, a DEFINITE sign. Which sign?/Which one?   "The sign **in Chinese and English**").

Again, the concept of "the" applies to plural nouns as well:

The signs *are in Chinese and English.*

(Notice that you're talking about SPECIFIC signs.   Which signs?/Which ones?   "The signs **in Chinese and English."**   Notice, again, how the plural impacts the verb; "is" becomes "are").

I would strongly advise you to go over these examples several times until you get "a feel" for the meaning of each individual sentence. These sentences offer you striking examples of the use of "**the**," examples that you can easily "see" and, I trust, begin to perceive the distinction.

Again, take it a step further

As with our everyday practice with "a," I would encourage you to practice "the" without paper and pen, no matter where you are, no matter what you are doing.

While on public transportation, you might think to yourself:

Most of the people on this train are on their smartphones.

Why "**the** people?"   Because you're talking about specific people,
"the people **on this train.**"

While walking down the street, you might say to yourself:

All the stores in this neighborhood are open late every night.

Why "**the** stores?"   Because you're referring to particular stores, "the
stores **in this neighborhood.**"

While in a restaurant, you might think to yourself:

The food *in this restaurant is inexpensive, but good.*

Why "the food?"   Because you're speaking about a definite food, "the
food **in this restaurant.**"

You could practice these simple, but highly effective, exercises
effortlessly anywhere.   I can assure you that if you do, they will
greatly help you to advance in your understanding—and use—of "**the**."
Nothing to buy, nothing to download, just you and your surroundings,
just you and your awareness.   What could be easier, more natural for
your learning and progress?   And, of equal importance, you are
learning how to learn.   You will be linking English to your everyday
life, just as you'll be doing when you live in an English-speaking
country.

You will be amazed at your progress when you give yourself the opportunity to use the reality—and your imagination—around you, when you give yourself the opportunity to use your innate (linguistic) learning ability.   Please keep in mind that we all have an innate (linguistic) learning ability.   If this were not true, none of us would have learned our mother tongue.   So, let us use our natural, intuitive ability to become successful learners.   Let us carefully consider Albert Einstein's perception:

The intuitive mind is a sacred gift, and the rational mind is a faithful servant.   We have created a society that honors the servant and has forgotten the gift.

Linking English to your daily experience

As aforementioned, these exercises are powerful as they show you the difference between "a" and "the" in situations that you can easily perceive in your daily life.   In this approach to learning, "a/an" and "the" are not grammar rules that you have laboriously studied but—more likely than not—have not really understood.   Again in the above exercise, you are, in essence, linking English to the reality around you; you are linking English to your experience.   Of equal importance, you are learning how to use them; you are getting "a feel" for how English "thinks."

Again, I would venture to say, dear student—and please forgive me for repeating it yet again—that if I had a dollar for every time one of my Chinese students omitted "the" in speaking or writing, I'd be one of the richest men in the world!   Please believe me, I do not exaggerate.   This mistake, as with plurals and omitting "a" occurs repeatedly in Chinese students' speaking and writing, no matter their level of proficiency, no matter how high their test scores.   Please keep in mind that these concepts of English are crucial to your being clearly and correctly understood.   Please keep in mind that "The 4 Golden Keys" keep English standing up, erect.   Without them, English collapses.   As suggested above, consider them carefully, practice them until they make sense to you.   This, inevitably, will lead to mastery!

Insights into Successful Learning 2

Bicycles and chopsticks

Allow me to put this simple question to you: Were you able to ride your bike the first time you got on it?   Of course not!   You had to learn how to balance yourself.   Remember how "unnatural" it felt to you?   With practice, however, it became second nature.   It no longer feels strange to you; it's no longer difficult.   You now jump on your bike without thinking twice!   Though you probably don't remember, you once had the very same challenge in learning to use chopsticks! Again, with repeated practice, it became second nature to you; it's no longer difficult.   You now pick up your chopsticks and use them with infinite ease!   Well, it's no different in speaking English.   With practice, the "unnatural/difficult" final [s], [z] and [əz] sound—or, for that matter, any new aspect of English, be it a grammatical structure or pronunciation—will become second nature to you, just like learning to ride a bike, just like learning to use chopsticks!   BUT, YOU HAVE TO PRACTICE IT, to make it a part of yourself, just as you made balancing a bike and using chopsticks a part of yourself.   It simply involves the decision—on your part—to make it a priority in your learning, and then to practice it until you master it.   Believe me, you

can do it!

What the ABCs teach us

Please consider that an ABC—an American Born Chinese—

will, most likely, be bilingual in Chinese and English.   There will be

no "foreign" accent in either language.   Her Chinese and English

pronunciation, her correct use of grammatical structures will essentially

be that of a native speaker.   What's this phenomenon telling us?   It's

telling us that whether we are Chinese or American—or Italian, Dutch,

or Greek etc.—we all have the innate intelligence to learn the structures

that the new language is asking us to use; we all have the same muscles

in our mouths, our throats, our lips, etc. to produce the sounds that any

language—whether it's our native language or a new language—is

asking us to make.   In other words, THE ABILITY IS IN ALL OF

US; we only have to access it.   We accessed it in learning our mother

tongue though we don't remember it.   Now, in learning English, we

are being asked to access it again.   This simple explanation, I trust,

will aid you in gaining a new view in learning English, will aid you in opening your mind to your potential, will aid you in expanding your understanding, in changing your perception.

If you keep this simple truth in mind, you will find that what you once thought was, "difficult" is only "different" and, thus, easier to access.   I feel that this perspective—this attitude of mind—is well worth your careful consideration.   It could very well open worlds to you!

Naysayers

I would also caution you, dear student, about naysayers who will expound about the brain and its inability to learn language after a certain age.   This attitude, in my opinion, breeds limitations.   No progress in any human endeavor has ever been made by stressing limitations.   We should view life, our lives, in terms of possibilities, not in terms of limitations—or what else are living and learning for? Allow me to quote the wisdom of the British poet, Robert Browning (1812-1889):

A man's reach should always exceed his grasp

or what's a heaven for?

Concept 4

Golden Key 4: Tense *(The action word—the verb—has the power!)*

Which word expresses time?

The essential idea is this: WHICH WORD IN AN ENGLISH SENTENCE OR QUESTION EXPRESSES TIME? A correct understanding of the answer to this question is crucial to your mastery of English. I do not exaggerate!

Let's investigate what I mean. In Chinese, "the time word" ("yesterday," "tomorrow," "next year," etc.)—AKA the adverb—alone indicates time, while "the action word" ("go," "sing," "write," etc.) remains the same, does not change.

This contrasts sharply with English where "the action word" ("go," "sing," "write," etc.)—aka the verb—EXPRESSES TIME AND CHANGES!

We might rephrase this by saying that in Chinese "THE TIME WORD" HAS THE POWER, whereas in English, "THE ACTION WORD" HAS THE POWER. This is another significant difference between English and Chinese and one which deserves your very careful attention and consideration.

It's impact on your English

Let's take a look at how this grammatical difference negatively impacts your English.   Chinese students, when speaking and writing English, tend to use ONLY the present tense!   Why?   Because it's a Chinese grammatical structure!   It's what you intrinsically know as native speakers of Chinese.   As a result, when referring to the past in English, Chinese students tend to use the present tense, adding "a time word," such as "yesterday"—at the beginning of the sentence—to indicate that their meaning is in the past, e.g., "Yesterday, I go shopping."

As we've seen before, the Chinese speaker, in spite of his numerous years of studying English, has the tendency to attach English words to Chinese grammar!   Result: 1) poor communication, 2) he stays stuck in Chinese English while leaving his native speaker of English confused.

In like manner, when referring to the future, Chinese students tend, once again, to use the present tense, plus "a time word," such as "tomorrow"—at the beginning of the sentence—to indicate that their

meaning is in the future, e.g., "Tomorrow, I go shopping."   Again,

Chinese grammar with English words!   Again, this grammatical

structure confuses their native English speakers and readers, impeding

clear communication.

Chinese can uses only the present tense because it relies

principally on "the time word" to signal time.   English, on the other

hand, relies principally on changing "the action word"/the verb to

signal time.   *(You may have learned—i.e., memorized—all the verb*

tenses in English, the regular as well as the irregular verbs, but, dear

student, you tend to revert to your native Chinese grammatical

structures when speaking and writing English!) Please understand

that I am not criticizing you.   I'm simply attempting to point out to

you what you do, attempting, as indicated above, to heighten your

awareness so that you can correct yourself, so that you can expand your

way of thinking, i.e., open your mind to a different way of thinking.

Please remember that learning a new language requires a change in

perception, a change in mindset.   No change in mindset equals no true

learning.   Let us remember that the very essence of learning—be it

English or math or calligraphy—is change.   As we have discussed, learning helps us to change, to become better, more aware, more understanding human beings.

Further investigations into how English and Chinese indicate tense

In this investigation of tense, we will use the past tense as our model as it succinctly demonstrates the differences in how English and Chinese express time.   Let's take a look at two more examples that readily reveal the differences in how English and Chinese express time.

Example 1:

Chinese says,

>   ***Last night****, I study.*

>   *or,*

>   *I last night study.*

English says,

>   *I **studied** last night.*

Notice that in the Chinese sentence, the time word ("last night") stands at the beginning of the sentence to indicate immediately the time of the action.   The action word ("study") is unchanged; it remains the same.

However, in the English sentence—and this warrants your careful consideration—the action word ("study") has changed and stands at the beginning of the sentence to indicate immediately the time of the action.   Why?   BECAUSE IN ENGLISH THE ACTION WORD PRINCIPALLY DETERMINES AND EXPLAINS TIME.   In English, THE ACTION WORD IS THE POWER WORD.   The action word is the key word.   As regards time, the English action word/the verb is king!

Allow me also to point out that the Chinese English sentence ("Last night, I study.") is confusing and contradictory to the native English speaker.   Why?   Because "last night" immediately triggers—in the English ear—the past.   Yet, the Chinese speaker says "study" which triggers *now*!   How can this be?   As a result, the English listener is likely to misunderstand, to be confused.

Example 2:

Chinese says,

> **Last year,** he go to China.

English says,

> He **went to** China last year.

Notice that in the Chinese sentence the time word ("Last year") is right up front to indicate immediately the time of the action.   Notice too that the action word ("go") is unchanged; it has remained the same.

However, in the English sentence—and again this warrants your very careful observation—the action word ("went") has changed and is in the beginning of the sentence to indicate immediately the time of the action.

Allow me to point out again that the Chinese sentence ("Last year, he go to China.") is confusing and contradictory to the native English speaker.   Why?   Because "last year" immediately triggers— in the English ear—the past.   Yet, the Chinese speaker says "go" which triggers *now*!   How can this be?   As a result, the English listener is likely to misunderstand, to be confused.

A closer look

Among more advanced students, this mistake in tense (the time word + present tense) takes this form.

Example 1: (actual student sentence)

Yesterday, *I **write** email and find it **is** much easier.*

Notice how the student triggered the past by using the time word *"yesterday"* at the beginning of the sentence—just as in Chinese—then proceeded to finish his idea using the present tense ("write," "find," "is").   Forgive me, but, once again, this sentence is essentially Chinese grammar with English words!   The student should have said:

> *I **wrote** an email yesterday and **found** it **was** much easier.*

Now, that's English; now, that's alignment!   All the components of the sentence fit together, work together, allowing the listener—or reader—to understand with ease.   Notice, too, the placement of "yesterday" in the English sentence.   This is the natural, spontaneous placement of "the time word" that a native speaker of English would use to express his idea.   **Notice that it doesn't come at the beginning of the sentence, nor at the end.**

Example 2: (actual student sentence)

> ***At that time***, *I **feel** it **is** the right thing to do.*

Again, notice how the student triggered the past by using, stressing the time words "at that time" at the beginning of the sentence, then proceeded to finish her idea using the present tense ("feel," "is"). Again, just as in Chinese.   Again, dear student, English words attached to Chinese grammar!   The sentence should have been

expressed as:

*At that time, I **felt** it **was** the right thing to do.*

Now, that's English; now, that's harmony!   All the

components of the sentence fit together, work together, allowing the

listener—or reader—to understand with ease.

Example 3: (actual student sentence)

*He **was** the first person who **call** me and let me know what **happen**.*

Here, the student starts off on the right foot.   Wonderful!   He

correctly indicates the past by writing "was."   Unfortunately, it's

short-lived.   He soon reverts to his native Chinese grammatical

structure of using only the present tense ("call," "happen").   He should

have written:

*He **was** the first person who **called** me to let me know what **happened**.*

Now, yet again, that's English; now, that's being aligned with

English!   All the components of the sentence fit together, work

together, allowing the listener—or reader—to understand with ease.

Forgive me for repeating this, dear reader, but these student

sentences are essentially English words attached to Chinese grammar!

Please know that the native speaker of English will, most likely, understand what the Chinese speaker is trying to say, but there will often be miscommunication.   The native speaker will have to work harder to understand, to listen/read more closely, to "translate" in his mind what the Chinese speaker actually means.   This requires the native speaker to expend more energy, energy he may not be willing—or have the time—to expend.   He may even lose interest in the conversation or in the writing.   Result: frustration and misunderstanding for both listener and speaker, for both writer and reader.

The above student sentences blatantly reveal that the students have not grasped the concept of tense in English.   In spite of their many years of studying English, they remain "stuck to" their native Chinese grammatical structures.

Although this tendency is natural to learners of a second language (to a degree), it shows us that there has been no change in perception, no change in the student's pattern of thinking, no change in mindset.   Please keep in mind: NO CHANGE, NO TRUE LEARNING.   But please remember, you have the ability to change yourself.   These sentences are showing us—may I say, shouting at us?—what you have to work on to gain mastery of English.

Therefore, keep in mind the importance of tense in English.   I do not exaggerate when I say that failure to use tense correctly will result in a breakdown in communication between you and your English-speaking listener and reader.

An important reminder

Thus, once again, it's important that you keep in mind that English is not a translation of Chinese.   I know I've said this repeatedly, but I repeat it because it is that important!   As we have previously pointed out, English is not a word-for-word translation of Chinese, just as Chinese is not a word-for-word translation of English. (This holds true for any language we learn).   In fact, the essence of this book is to show you, dear student, how English "thinks" and "speaks" differently from Chinese, to show you the major areas where English thinks and expresses itself differently from Chinese so that you can focus on them, expand your pattern of thinking, and thus become competent speakers and writers of English.

A worthwhile reflection

It's interesting to note that—essentially—we have the same situation here with tense that we had with plurals, i.e., English and Chinese stressing different parts of speech to convey meaning.

With plurals, Chinese stresses the adjective, English stresses the noun.   With tense, Chinese stresses the adverb, English, the verb. Please ponder this carefully.   It will open your thought to correct English and the wonder of language.

Further Considerations on "The 4 Golden Keys"

A major discovery for you!

At this point in our investigations, I would like to point out to you that we have just made a major discovery.   (Please keep in mind that investigations always lead to discoveries!   This point is crucial to your learning).   What, then, is this discovery?

In Golden Keys 1, 2 and 3, we are talking principally about English NOUNS and in Golden Key 4, we are talking principally about English VERBS.   English NOUNS AND VERBS, not English adjectives, nor adverbs, nor prepositions, etc.   ONLY NOUNS AND VERBS!   In other words, the very heart of the Chinese student's challenge—in learning English—centers on using English nouns and verbs correctly.   (Yes, I admit that there are other challenges, but they pale in comparison).   We might say it this way: "The 4 Golden Keys" deserve your complete attention in mastering English.   Remember they are the foundation that keep English standing up.   Everything you say or write will involve "The 4 Golden Keys."   Everything!

So, why—you may well ask—is it a major discovery? Because it is a gigantic step forward in any learning process to become aware of our major weaknesses.   Once we know our weaknesses, we know what we have to concentrate on!   We now have a definite direction.   We can be assured that we are traveling down the right road.   We are no longer floundering, groping, wondering—perhaps, even worrying about—what to do to make progress.   We now know where our major focus should be.   What a relief!

So, may I suggest that you diligently concentrate on nouns and verbs, no matter your level of proficiency.   Without a doubt, they hold a major key to your mastering English.   Remember then to always FOCUS ON THE CHANGES THAT NOUNS AND VERBS UNDERGO IN AN ENGLISH SENTENCE OR QUESTION.   Keep in mind that in English, nouns and verbs change, in Chinese they don't.   Be sure then that you observe carefully how they change.   This is a vital point for your success in English.   Its importance cannot be over-stressed.

Therefore, be on your guard: DO NOT SKIM OVER A SENTENCE TO GET ONLY THE MEANING.   Doing so will cost you; it will undermine your progress.   Please remember that "how" a sentence is expressed is as important to you as "what" it means.

Watering your garden

"The 4 Golden Keys" are new concepts for you.   As they do not exist in Chinese, they will require regular "watering."   No gardener or farmer plants seeds and then forgets them.   He knows that they require regular watering and care.   It's no different in learning English.   Regular "watering" is required in the form of meaningful practice.   Make "The 4 Golden Keys" a priority in all your investigations and watch your progress soar!   Again, I ask you to trust me in this.   Please allow me to remind you that mastering the concepts presented in this book will serve you far better than memorizing grammar rules and lists of vocabulary words!

Strengthening your understanding of plurals, "a/an," "the" and the tense

As you now see that "The 4 Golden Keys" (plurals "a/an," "the" and the tense) are crucial concepts of English for the Chinese student, seek every opportunity to heighten your awareness of them.   I repeat, please don't skim over them as if they didn't exist, as if they were unimportant, because they are, in fact, extremely important.

As we have recommended when practicing plurals, you might again—when reading—circle or highlight every "a," "an," "the," and verb tense as well.   You might approach it as follows:

Example 1: If you read

I sent him an email yesterday,

circle or highlight "sent" and "an email" Then, ask yourself, "Why did they say 'sent'?"   "Oh yes, I see.   They're talking about yesterday, which is in the past, thus 'sent.' " Ask yourself, "Why did they say, 'an email?' "   "Oh yes, I see now."   "They're talking about **one** email, thus; 'an email' "

Example 2: If you read,

He gave me a kiss before he left home,

circle or highlight "gave," "a kiss" and "left."   Then, ask yourself, "Why did they say, 'gave,' 'left'?"   "Oh yes, I see, the action is in the past, it already happened, therefore, 'gave,' 'left.' " Then, ask yourself, "Why did they say, 'a kiss?' " "Oh yes, I understand.It's like 'a pen,''a dog," "a cafe," etc.   They're talking about **one** kiss, thus "a kiss."

Example 3: If you read,

All my friends are going to the party,

circle or highlight, "friends," "are going to," "the party."   Then, ask yourself, "Why did they say, 'friends?' "   "Oh yes, I see.   There was more than one 'friend,' thus, 'friends.' "   "Why did they say, 'are going to'? "   "Oh, I see they are talking about the future; thus, 'are going to.' "   "Why did they say, 'the party'? "   "Oh yes, I see now they are referring to a specific party, thus, 'the party.' "   Practice this regularly to reinforce your understanding.   If you find it daunting to work on all "The 4 Golden Keys" at once, then work on them individually, one at a time, at your own pace.   In other words, work on plurals until you feel you have a handle on them, then proceed to "a/an," then "the," then "tense."   In this way, you will easily work your way through all "The 4 Golden Keys."

By questioning yourself, as shown above, you will grow in understanding.   You will begin to see that plurals, "a," "an," "the," and the tense are essential concepts of English, that they play a major role in accurate, clear communication.   And, be sure not to limit your practice to just reading.   Keep your ears open when listening to native speakers of English, whether in conversation or on TV or in a movie. Listen carefully for the plurals, "a/an," "the" and the tense.   They will always be present!

I trust you can now understand why I refer to "The 4 Golden Keys" as the "foundation" of English for Chinese speakers.   I might add that they are the very heart of English for the Chinese student.   Be alert to these important concepts of English in speaking, listening, reading and writing.   The more you pay attention to them, the more they will make sense to you, the more you will find them easier to use. You will begin to use them without thinking twice.   You will begin to use them naturally.   What once felt "foreign" to you will no longer feel so.   They will have become second nature.   Let us always keep in mind Lao Tzu's (604 BCE-531 BCE) brilliant wisdom:

Knowledge is a treasure, but practice is the key to it.

A solid foundation

Mastering "The 4 Golden Keys" will—without a doubt—put you in harmony with what English really is; they will help you to gain a true "feel" for English.   They will put the right "architectural drawings" in your hands.   The Chinese student who puts his attention on these four concepts will be building a solid foundation in speaking, writing and understanding English.   Without a mastery of these concepts, you are building your house on sand.

So, please put your attention on mastering "The 4 Golden Keys"—no matter what your level of proficiency—so that you build your "home" on a solid foundation, a foundation that will properly support you. ***Please keep in mind that these concepts are as important for the advanced student, the working professional as for the beginning and intermediate student.*** Please indulge me for repeating that I have tutored Chinese MD and PhD candidates who struggle in expressing themselves clearly in their professional lives as well as in writing their dissertations, simply because they have not mastered these concepts. Without this all-important foundation, your "home" will, most likely, cave in on you.

As stated above, the grammar points of "The 4 Golden Keys" do not exist in Chinese. To master them, you will have to open your mind to a new way of perceiving the world, you will have to change your pattern of thinking. Be patient with yourself; take your time. With awareness and practice, they will become part of you, just like learning to ride a bicycle, just like learning to use chopsticks. Please trust me in this.

Not insignificant matters

And, please bear with me as I—once again—repeat that if I had a dollar for every time I corrected a Chinese student in these four areas, I would be one of the wealthiest individuals in the world!   I do not say this to ridicule, but to impress upon you the importance that "The 4 Golden Keys" have in your success as competent speakers and writers of English.

Plurals, "a/an," "the," and the tense may seem insignificant from your Chinese perspective, but please believe me when I tell you that from an English perspective, they aren't!   Again, speaking and writing without "The 4 Golden Keys" strongly indicates to your native English-speaker that you don't speak English well.   Please keep in mind that plurals, "a/an," "the," and the tense are vital concepts in English.   They impact the entire language and determine whether or not the Chinese speaker is accurately understood.   They are, without a doubt, essential principles of English.   I do not exaggerate!

A word to the wise! 1

Although I've outlined the uses of plurals, "a/an," "the," and the tense, please keep in mind that THERE WILL ALWAYS BE AN

EXCEPTION TO THE RULE, no matter what the topic!   ALWAYS!

Such is the nature of language, such is the nature of life itself!   Be

careful then not to make a discovery into a rigid rule.   Think of "rules"

as guidelines.   This simple advice will help you to maintain an open,

flexible attitude in all your learning.

Insights into Successful Learning 3

Gaining freedom

Allow me to reiterate that the concepts presented in this book involve EXPANDING YOUR PRESENT WAY OF THINKING. This is the very essence of all learning.   The (English) concepts that are presented within these pages are outside your (Chinese) experience. Thus, you will have to open your mind to them.   Your task, then, is to integrate this new English "world" with your Chinese "world."   Like learning how to ride your bike and learning how to use chopsticks, it will require a bit of effort—and practice—on your part, but you will eventually get it!

These concepts will help to free you from having only a Chinese mindset.   They will help to free you from being culture bound.   All of us, no matter what our nationality, are—to varying degrees—culture bound.   Learning a second language helps to free us from our native cultural perspectives.   We begin to see that there are other ways of viewing the world, other ways of viewing life itself. Language learning broadens our horizons.   This is one of its major lessons, a lesson, I feel, that should be a part of all our investigations.

As previously mentioned, most language students—no matter their nationality—tend to assume that the new language, with its grammar, pronunciation, etc., is the same as their mother tongue.   In our case, Chinese students mistakenly tend to "think" that English conforms to Chinese grammar and pronunciation.   Again, I repeat, nothing could be farther from the truth.   Language simply does not work that way.

Americans learning Chinese would, likewise, face challenges in expanding their understanding Americans learning Chinese would, likewise, have "blind spots."   Let us keep in mind that it's a universal human issue; it has nothing to do with nationality.

Changing and expanding our way of thinking is at the very root of all successful language learning.   Let us remember that learning is about change, learning involves changing ourselves and gaining freedom.   I repeat, be patient with yourself, take your time.   You can do it!

The vital role of mistakes in learning

The concepts addressed in this book are based on my firsthand observations of the mistakes that Chinese students tend to make.   As is the case when anyone makes a mistake, students are, as a rule, unaware of making them.   (After all, no one makes a mistake on purpose!)   So, what happens?   They make the same mistakes again and again.   My purpose, then, is to help you become aware of your mistakes.   This book is largely based on the premise that once you become aware of your mistakes—your weaknesses—you have only to put your attention on them—to focus on them—and through practice, correct them.   Once you become aware of your mistakes, you are halfway on the road to mastery!

Your mistakes play a vital role in expanding your thinking, they play a major role in pointing you in the right direction, and, subsequently, an important role in your success.   I know this may sound strange to you, but it's true.   Your mistakes are essential components to mastering English, IF YOU USE THEM CONSTRUCTIVELY.   Believe it or not, your mistakes are your guides; they signal to you the areas you need to concentrate on so that you can make progress.

Dr. Gattegno put it this way and I will never forget it.   He pointed out that when we were learning how to walk, we stumbled and fell many times before we learned how to balance ourselves correctly.

Each fall seemed like a "mistake," yet, it wasn't.   Through each fall, through each "mistake," we were learning, we were teaching ourselves— though we don't remember it—how to maintain our balance and take a step forward.   In other words, we were learning through our awareness—through the "mistakes" we made—how to correct ourselves so that we could stand erect and walk!   The process is the same in whatever we undertake to learn, i.e., we learn via our mistakes; we learn via our awareness.

Therefore, welcome your mistakes and learn from them. Don't blacken them out in pen or pencil as if they didn't exist.   Don't sweep them under the carpet, don't hide them as a source of embarrassment.   Mistakes are your friends.   Remember that no true learning can take place without MAKING MISTAKES and—if you are wise—learning from them.   Mistakes point the way to your success!

Investigating the word "mistake"

I love the English word "mistake" because it says—reveals— exactly what it means.   If we take a closer look at the word "mistake," we discover that it's comprised of two parts: the prefix "mis" and the word "take."

The prefix "mis" carries the meaning of "wrong/incorrectly" and "take" carries the meaning of "understand."   Thus, when we say, *"I made a mistake,"* we actually mean, "I wrongly understood," or "I incorrectly understood."   In essence, we thought it was one thing, but discover—we come to realize—that it's other than we thought.   No big deal!   Now we know what we have to do.   Now we know what we have to change—in ourselves—to come to the correct understanding.

The beauty of a mistake is that it gives birth to contrast.   I—as a learner—can say to myself, "Oh, I thought 'He studies in U.S.' was correct English, but now—through becoming aware of my "mis-take," and the contrast it offers—I see that 'He studies in **the** U.S.' is the correct English."   How wonderful!   Now, I know and can move forward—take a step forward—with confidence.   My mistake showed me the correct English.   I'm making progress!

Likewise, I can say to myself, *"Oh, I thought 'Didn't I told you?'   was correct English, but now—through becoming aware of what I "mis-took," and the contrast it offers—I see that 'Didn't I tell you?,' is the correct English."   How wonderful!   Now, I know for sure and can move forward.   I'm one step closer to mastering English! My mistake taught me the correct English.   I'm making progress.

What a freeing learning expericnce!   Essentially, I "mistook," I misunderstood (I wrongly understood), I misinterpreted (I incorrectly interpreted) the point in question.   I didn't commit a felony; my mistake is not unalterable.   I simply "mistook" something. What a relief, then, to finally know what is correct!   We are now freed and can thus progress on our path of learning and growing.   Please remember: WE CAN CHANGE!   And this change that takes place in our—inner—selves is at the very heart of learning, the very heart of our new view.

Therefore, welcome your mistakes, learn from your mistakes. Please do not berate yourself for making mistakes.   They are nothing to be ashamed of.   Everyone makes mistakes!   They are an essential, integral part of your learning, of making progress, of life!   Mistakes are pointing you in the right direction.   Mistakes are pointing you toward mastery.   A mistake is just a mistake and can be corrected and learned from.   Confucius knew this when he stated,

Be not ashamed of mistakes and thus make them crimes.

So, let's remember that: MISTAKES TEACH US! MISTAKES ARE OUR TEACHERS!   MISTAKES ARE OUR FRIENDS!   MISTAKES ARE OUR GUIDES!   MISTAKES LEAD US TO THE RIGHT ANSWER!   Maintaining this attitude—this vital insight—will definitely facilitate your progress.

"Knowing about" vs "knowing how to do"

So often we overlook the fact that "knowing about" something and "knowing how to do" something are two very different experiences.   The former is passive; the latter is active, and it is active learning that we strive for in our investigations.   Learning a language, like learning how to play a musical instrument, is about knowing how to do it.   It requires, by its very nature, active learning, active participation.   It requires coordination.   You can study from textbooks until you're blue in the face, but you will not learn how to play the piano until you actually sit down and play it.   It's no different, dear student, in learning to speak English.   Let us then focus on "knowing how to do."   Let's focus on active learning in the "here and now," so that you can become competent speakers and writers of English.

The Zen Buddhist, John Daido Loori, wisely guides us when he points out:

We choose knowing over direct experience.

Let us then pursue the direct experience in learning English!

A music lesson and learning English

This being the case, i.e., "knowing how to do," I would ask you to kindly consider the dynamics of a music lesson.   We can learn a great deal from the model of a music lesson because learning a language is very much like learning how to play a musical instrument; it involves active participation and coordination.   As we have seen, language is alive, breathing, flexible, moving in the air, just like music.

Imagine, if you will, the following scenario.   Your music teacher shows you a piano, he lifts up the lid and shows you the piano's inner construction: the hammers, the strings, the bridge, the tuning pins, the soundboard, etc. You, then, proceed to memorize the names of these inner mechanisms.   He, subsequently, shows you the keyboard and you, again, proceed to memorize all the black and white keys.   He continues in his instruction, showing you score after score of sheet music, many of which, you—once again—dutifully memorize. Having "learned" all he has taught you, you then take and pass challenging, standardized written piano exams.

Imagine further that in spite of this rigorous training, you have not once had the opportunity to actually sit down and play the piano! Though I may exaggerate—a bit—is this not what, all too often, happens in English classes, where students learn about English, but have little opportunity to speak it. To avoid this soulless approach to "learning," attempt to base your investigations on a real music lesson where you are actually playing "your instrument." i.e., actually speaking and listening to English.   Provide yourself with every possible opportunity to play the music, not just talk about it!   In other words, provide yourself every possible opportunity to speak English, not just passively memorize it!

"Practice makes better"

Practice then is the key to success in anything you undertake to master.   When you listen to an accomplished musician, you're listening to hours, days, months, years of daily practice.   When you view a beautiful example of Chinese calligraphy, you're viewing the fruit of regular practice.   It's the same, dear student, with learning to speak and write English fluently.   "Practice makes better!"   It's as

simple and uncomplicated as that.

Xunzi (c.310-c.235 B.C.E.) in his timeless wisdom tells us,

I hear and I forget.   I see and I remember. I do and I understand.

Part IV

Expressing It Correctly in English

The following concepts (Concepts 5 through 11) discuss

additional—major— grammatical areas where Chinese students tend to

repeatedly make mistakes.   As we investigate these areas, you will

discover that—like "The 4 Golden Keys"—these English grammar

concepts do not exist in the Chinese language.   So, what happens?   I

trust you know the answer by now.   That's right, you've got it, the

Chinese student will attach English words to his native Chinese

grammatical structures!

Your English is bound to improve tremendously if you focus

diligently on these key concepts and integrate them into your spoken

and written English.   As with "The 4 Golden Keys," we will carefully investigate these concepts so as to put you in alignment with everyday American English.

Concept 5

Asking questions correctly

An English question, please

I would venture to say that the majority of the Chinese students with whom I work do not ask a question correctly in English.   I do not exaggerate, the majority!   (Please know that I do not say this to insult or ridicule.   I say it to bring it to your awareness so that you can focus on it, correct it and thus master it.   Please understand that asking questions correctly is an essential element in speaking English correctly).

In asking a question in English, students, almost always, follow the Chinese pattern.   That is to say, they use intonation.   Using intonation to ask a question IS NOT THE STANDARD WAY OF ASKING A QUESTION IN ENGLISH.   Again, it's Chinese English. It is true that English—in certain situations—uses intonation to ask a question, but it's not the usual way.   The intonation question carries a different meaning.   Let's investigate!

If, for example, a native speaker of English wants to clarify, to satisfy a slight doubt that she may have, she may use intonation in asking a question.   In other words, the native speaker is seeking confirmation of his or her uncertainty.   She is essentially saying, "I want to be sure I understand you correctly."   Let's take a look at a few examples:

Example 1: When a native speaker of English says, "You're leaving at 5?" she essentially means, "I'm pretty sure that you're leaving at 5, but I'm asking you because I want to be sure that I've understood you correctly."   Thus, she asks the question using intonation.

Example 2: When a native speaker of English says, "You graduated from the University of Rochester?", he's under the impression that you graduated from the University of Rochester, but wants confirmation of his minor doubt.   The question that uses intonation usually carries the feeling of "Is that right?"   "Am I right?" "Have I understood you correctly?"   Thus, he asks the question using intonation.

In most other cases, however, an English question is asked by using: "do," "does," "did," "would," "will," "should," "can," etc., or by inverting the subject and the verb ("Is he?", "Were they?").

Chinese English questions vs English questions

Let's investigate a few examples of Chinese English (intonation questions) and how the questions should be expressed in everyday, standard English.

Example 1: The average ESL student will ask,

"You like Chinese food?"

(Take a moment now to reflect on this.   Is this not the way you ask a question in Chinese?) The native speaker of English, of course, understands the "question," but, as stated above, it is NOT CORRECT ENGLISH.   It's not standard, everyday spoken English. It's a Chinese grammatical pattern with English words!   The correct English question is:

"Do you like Chinese food?"

Example 2: The Chinese ESL student will ask,

"You are leaving tomorrow?"

(Again, take a moment to reflect on this.   Is this not the way you ask a question in Chinese?) Yes, the native speaker of English understands the "question," but, it's not correct English.   Again, it's a Chinese grammatical pattern with English words!   The correct English question is:

"Are you leaving tomorrow?"

Example 3: The Chinese speaker will ask,

"She went to Vermont?"

(Again, please take a moment to reflect on this.   Is this not the way you ask a question in Chinese?) I repeat, the native speaker of English understands the "question," but it's not correct English.   It's a Chinese grammatical pattern with English words!   The correct question is:

"Did she go to Vermont?"

This is a major concept, a major pattern in everyday English and one you should focus on if you wish to gain mastery of English.

Wh-questions impacted

Using intonation to ask questions, in turn, negatively impacts your ability to ask a wh-question correctly.   It is any wonder, then, that Chinese students tend to phrase a wh-questions as follows:

Why I should do that?

Where he lives in the States?

What she can do?

When they are coming?

These wh-questions, however, should be phrased as follows:

*Why **should** I do that?*

*Where **does he** live in the States?*

*What **can she** do?*

*When **are they** coming?*

Please note that if you ask a basic English question correctly, ("Did you find your wallet?"), you will have no difficulty in asking a wh-question correctly ("Where did you find your wallet?").   One logically fits into the other.   As the English expression states, "They go hand-in-hand."   Kindly consider this vital point—this grammatical pattern—in the following questions:

Example 1: **Does she take** the bus to work?

easily and correctly becomes:

*Why **does she take** the bus to work?*

Example 2: Are **they going** on vacation?

easily and correctly becomes:

*When **are they going** on vacation?*

Example 3: **Is he studying** in the States?

easily and correctly becomes:

*What's **he studying** in the States?*

Example 4: **Would she like** to go?

easily and correctly becomes:

Where would she like to go?

Example 5: **Did they study** together?

easily and correctly becomes:

*Why **did they study** together?*

or

*When **did they study** together?*

or

*Where **did they study** together?*

Notice how the basic structure of the question remains the same.   Notice how it fits harmoniously into the wh-question.   This demonstrates that each aspect of language is integrated, that each aspect of language is related to another, that each aspect of language is linked to another, that each aspect of language impacts another.   Just like life itself; it's all integrated!

Mastery through active practice

This mistake in asking an English question correctly is another case where the Chinese student has studied English grammar, is familiar with the concept, but reverts to the pattern of his native Chinese grammar when speaking and writing.   The English pattern of asking questions—which does not come naturally to the Chinese student—will only be mastered if you practice it regularly.   Poring over grammar rules, filling in the blanks, etc.,—all of which I'm sure you have done—will not ensure your success in speaking English. Therefore, allow this concept of English to enter your awareness.   Be mindful, be sure that you practice it in both your spoken and written English.   Listen for it when conversing with native speakers.   Failure to do so may result in your passing standardized tests, but not speaking or understanding English well!   Please keep in mind: Practice makes better.

Answering questions: a round peg in a round hole

ANSWERING A QUESTION correctly is as important as ASKING A QUESTION correctly.   Kindly consider this point in the following scenarios.

If you ask a Chinese student of English,

"Do you understand?",

she will simply answer either,

"Yes" or "No."

(This, of course, is acceptable).   If you then ask her, *"Yes, what?"*, she will respond, *"Yes, I understand."*   THIS IS NOT CORRECT ENGLISH; this response is not in alignment with what English really is.   A native speaker of English—when asked the same question—would spontaneously answer, *"Yes, I do."*   Ah, now that's the spirit of English; it's a round peg in a round hole, not a square peg in a round hole!   In other words, it fits!   It's in alignment, it harmonizes!   This is English in alignment with itself.   This is the speaker in harmony with English!   And this alignment, dear student, should be your constant aim in learning English.

Let's take a look at another example to illustrate this point. Ask a Chinese student,

"Are you sure?"

and he will answer,

"Yes" or "No."

(Again, this is acceptable).   If, however, you then ask him, *"Yes, what?"*   Sure as the sun will rise tomorrow, he will answer, *"Yes, I am sure."*   Again, this is NOT THE RIGHT USE OF

ENGLISH.   A native speaker would spontaneously answer, "Yes, I am" or *"No, I'm not."*   Again, what English really is and sweet harmony!

Although the native speaker of English would spontaneously answer, "Yes, I do," or *"No, I don't,"* it is equally possible, as indicated above, that he might simply answer *"Yes"* or *"No."*   Of course!   My point in this discussion is to show that the Chinese student, as a rule, is not in harmony with the spirit of English, he is not aligned with what English really is, which ultimately impacts his—accurate— understanding.   Please understand, dear reader, that I am nit-picking; I'm attempting to harmonize you with English, to help you gain the right view, to align you with living, breathing, correct English.

Upon a moment's reflection, you can now readily see that there is a direct correlation—a vital link, an alignment—between question and answer:

__Do__ you understand?

Yes, I __do__.

__Are__ you sure?

Yes, I __am__.

Question and answer are related, connected, linked; they are in harmony!

     At this point, let's take a look at an important characteristic of English that often escapes the ESL learner, an aspect of English that impacts the language in several important ways, that functions as a thread that runs throughout English, that unifies the language and reveals a way of expression that is unique to English.   I trust that the following simple examples will bring the importance of this singularly English mode of expression to light for all Chinese students of English. Let's investigate the following conversations:

> *Xing:* ***Did*** *you like the movie?*
>
> *David: Yes, I **did**.*
>
> *Xing:* ***Did*** *your roommate?*
>
> *David: Yes, he really **did**.*
>
> *Xing: How about your parents?*
>
> *David: No, they **didn't**.   They objected to the violence.*

     Observe, the main verb ("like") is used only once in the entire conversation; the meaning of the conversation being carried by the word "did," which was introduced in the initial question.

Here is another example to help clarify this characteristic of English as well as to show its function in everyday English:

Jonathan: ***Do*** *you eat junk food?*

Patrick: *Almost never,* ***do*** *you?*

Jonathan: *No, I* ***don't***, *but my brother* ***does***.

Notice, again, how "do," "don't," "does" carry the meaning of the conversation, not the verb "to eat."   In other words, the entire conversation is carried by the word "do" which was introduced in the initial question.

Here is yet another example of this phenomenon in English:

Sue*:* ***Would*** *you like to go?*

Ron: *I sure* ***would***!

Sue: ***Would*** *you mind picking me up?*

Ron: *No,* ***I'd*** *be glad to.*

Notice how **"would"**—not the verb, "like"—carries the meaning of the conversation.

This grammatical concept—without a doubt—is particular to English and, once again, reveals its spirit.   This unique feature of English plays a major role in clear communication and comprehension and will, if practiced, greatly help you to be in alignment with native speakers of English.

Following are additional examples in which "do," " did," " is," " was," " will," " would," etc.   play an important role in revealing meaning and the spirit of English:

*I live in Philadelphia, but my sister **doesn't.***

*I wish she **did**!*

*My father never buys anything online, but I **do**.*

*Stuart **had** to cram for his finals, but Susan didn't.*

*Joyce **is** planning on going, but Bob **isn't** .*

And here's an example I heard on the train—just the other day on the way to school—between two women sitting behind me:

Woman 1*: I think she changed her name, **didn't** she?*

Woman 2*: Yes, I think she **did**.*

Ah, dear student, the spirit of English—and, may I add— the beautiful, unique spirit of English!

Major gears

As we have just seen, "do," "did," "is," "are," etc. are not only important in asking and answering questions, but are also linked to other important aspects of English.   Again, we can say that they are pivotal, having implications that are crucial to speaking and understanding English correctly, crucial to understanding the very spirit of English.   This grammatical feature of English could be likened to gears in a mechanical device where one gear impacts other gears, ultimately causing alignment and motion.   This time, however, the gears are: "do," "did," "is," "are,"   "would," etc.!   As in a mechanical device, all will run smoothly, if the gears are correctly positioned.   If they aren't, there will be problems.   It's the same with English.   Be sure then that you have a firm understanding of these "gears" so that you will be in harmony with what English really is!

Additional Considerations Regarding Questions

Phrasing a question for optimum learning

Here is another vital point about questions that warrants your careful attention: It is important that you know HOW TO ASK A QUESTION THAT WILL BEST SERVE YOUR LEARNING.   We might put it this way: It's important that you know HOW TO PHRASE A CONSTRUCTIVE QUESTION.   This may sound strange, but it isn't!   Allow me to explain.   I have found that many students either don't know how to ask a question that will best serve their progress or are afraid to ask questions.

Let's investigate!   When given the opportunity to ask a question, students tend to ask questions that are too general.   They will, for instance, ask "When do I use 'a' and when do I use 'the'?" or "When do I use 'in' and when do I use 'on'?"   Such questions are understandable, but are far too broad!   They will not serve you well. Even if your teacher answered them for you, your eyes—most likely— would soon glaze over because you couldn't "digest" all the information.   Most people couldn't!   Your teacher would have gone through the motions of answering the question, you would have gone through the motions of "listening," but, I venture to say, dear student, that little would have actually been learned. You might have learned something about the piano, but your fingers would have never touched the keyboard!

Thus, it's of prime importance that you ask a simpler, to-the-point question that reflects a real life use of English that will advance you in understanding. A good, to-the-point question would be:

*"Do you say, 'I had **a** good time.' or 'I had **the** good time?' "*

This type of question reveals that you are in touch with English, that you are listening, that you are reflecting on what you hear, or what you see. This type of question provides you with something concrete to work on, something that you and your teacher can sink your teeth into! Your teacher could then offer that *"I had **a** good time,"* is the correct—and the only—way to express the idea, that *"I had **the** good time"* is not only incorrect, but it doesn't exist! English always says, *"I had **a** good time."* This simple answer to this simple question leaves little room for confusion or misunderstanding. Upon learning the correct answer (*"I had **a** good time."*), you now know, you are no longer in doubt. Your simple—to the point—question has freed you. You can now move on, assured of the correct English.

Here's another example of a to-the-point question:

*" Do you say, 'I have to **reply** his email,'*

or

*'I have to **reply to** his email?' "*

Again, we have something concrete—to the point—to work on. This type of question reveals that you are in touch with the language, that you are reflecting on how English works.   Upon learning the correct answer ("I have to **reply to** his email.") from your teacher or a friend—or from a reputable dictionary—you now know, you are no longer in doubt.   Just as in the first example, the answer to this simple, pinpointed question leaves little room for confusion or misunderstanding.   The issue is settled once and for all.   You've taken a step forward; you've made progress!

By approaching questions in this format (*"Do you say _____ or do you say _____?,"* or any other pinpointed question, for that matter), you are phrasing a question that will best serve your learning. In essence, you are learning how to "look at" English, you are learning how to approach it.   You now have the right perspective.   You are working directly on the language as you find it.   You are redirecting your hypothetical—often too broad—grammar-rule focus to a here-and-now situation. You are seeing how English works, how English expresses itself, how English "speaks." You are freeing yourself from the self-defeating attitude of "getting-only-the-main-ideas" which, as we have noted, does not serve you. And, of equal importance, you are learning how to learn!

Kindly keep in mind that I am talking about a phrase, a part of a sentence, not a whole sentence, not necessarily isolated words. I'm suggesting that you pay attention to the word immediately before or after the noun or verb, e.g., "**a** good time," "reply **to**."

Equally important, you are freeing yourself from the erroneous mindset that all of English can be categorized—has to be categorized—into neatly, hard-and-fast packaged rules that have no exceptions. Such an attitude is unrealistic and limiting. Such an attitude is airtight, leaving no room for English—or you (!) —to breathe. It will result in impeding your progress.

However, by working as we have suggested, you will have a new view that will bring you closer to what English really is. This is a natural approach as you are learning how to reflect and to question intelligently. This approach will serve you in the classroom as well as in the future when you are in an English-speaking environment.   As in all natural, true learning, you are learning how to encounter the new and integrate it into your ever-expanding awareness.

Questions are golden opportunities for learning

Please keep in mind that it's of prime importance for your progress to ask questions if you do not understand or have a doubt about the matter at hand.   Let's not overlook that **asking questions— like making mistakes and learning from them—is an essential part of your learning.**   No true learning can take place without asking questions!   Its value cannot be overemphasized.   We, as humans, are always attempting—whether we articulate it or not—to understand the world around us, always attempting "to put the pieces together." Thus, it is only natural to have questions.   We all have questions, teachers and students alike, adults and children alike!   Whether in our personal lives, or in the classroom, each of us is confronted with the new, the "unknown,"—as Dr. Gattegno would express it—and, thus, are bound to have questions.   Please keep in mind that there's no shame in not knowing, in not understanding; therefore, there's no shame in asking a question.

If, at any given moment, you have a question or a doubt—that question, that uncertainty—should be expressed and answered. Once your question is answered, once your doubt is resolved, you arc, as we have previously discussed, set free to move on, to take the next step, to progress. However, if your question or doubt remains unanswered, you may get snagged and, perhaps, collide with the next new concept you encounter on your learning path, subsequently, falling behind. So, please make asking questions an essential part of your learning. The majority of your teachers will be delighted that you have. It readily shows them that you are involved in your learning. I can't imagine a teacher who would not welcome this active participation in his or her classroom!

Let's always keep in mind Ja'far-al Sadiq's (AD 702-765) insight:

Certainly, knowledge is a lock and its key is the question.

Please speak up

Therefore, if you have a question or a doubt, make it a point to ask your teacher. Forgive me, but experience has shown me that Chinese students tend to be reluctant to ask questions. Working with

Asian students has always been a pleasure.   Your respect for your teachers and for learning is unparalleled.   However, dear student, nothing is more frustrating for an American professor than to ask a class of Asian students, "Does anyone have any questions?" only to be confronted with absolute silence!   How can this be?   It's impossible to study a new language without having questions!   It's impossible to study anything without having questions!   It's impossible to be alive, living without having any questions!   It goes against the grain!   It goes against nature itself!

So, let me repeat that there's no shame in not knowing, no shame in asking a question if you don't understand, particularly in a classroom environment where the sole purpose is to question, to investigate, to learn.   I understand that this reluctance to ask a question may, in essence, be cultural, but, Chinese students preparing to study in the U.S.will meet with greater success if they are willing to—know how to—ask questions.   Their American teachers and professors, especially in their English classes, will expect it of them! Little else, dear student, can advance your learning more than having the self-confidence to ask a question.   It's as important as learning

"The 4 Golden Keys to English."   Doors will fly open for you; you will make progress.   Please do not shy away from asking questions.

Let me assure you that if you have a doubt, or are unclear about any aspect of English, you can be sure that many of your classmates have the same doubt!   Consequently, they too, will be enriched by the questions you ask, and, who knows, your questions may encourage them to participate in the discussion, or ask a question of their own! Again, I ask you to please trust me in this.

Client/lawyer; student/teacher

This reluctance to asking questions is akin to an individual seeking help from a lawyer, but not explaining his case!   Kindly consider the following scenario.   The client goes to the lawyer's office and the lawyer asks, "What's the matter?", "How can I help you?", but the client does not answer!   He sits in the chair, remaining silent. How can the lawyer help his client if the client is reluctant to answer the lawyer's questions, if the client is reluctant to express himself? Though this scenario may seem absurd, it's similar to what happens in our American classrooms where students don't ask questions.   How can your teachers help you, if you don't ask questions?   How can they guide you, if you don't question them?

Allow me to reiterate that asking questions is an essential component of learning.   In asking questions, you will be cultivating your natural abilities to learn; you will be "watering" your garden; you will better prepare yourself for your studies on American campuses. You will better prepare yourself for life!

Insights into Successful Learning 4

The relationship between grammatical structures and vocabulary

As indicated above, your English will improve tremendously if your primary focus is on its grammatical structures, not on its vocabulary.   I know this sounds backwards, but it isn't.   This different perspective will reveal to you how English "works," how English "thinks;" it will expand your way of thinking.   It will open your mind to what English really is.   (Please understand that I do not mean that vocabulary is unimportant.   Of course it's important, but it's not enough.   Its role is secondary to understanding and using grammatical structures).

Too often, students mistakenly stress vocabulary over grammar. They often think that it is necessary to memorize long lists of vocabulary in order to speak English.   Although vocabulary has an important role to play in language learning, PLEASE KNOW THAT MEMORIZING THE ENTIRE DICTIONARY FROM COVER TO COVER WILL NOT ENABLE YOU TO SPEAK ENGLISH CORRECTLY.   Such an perspective is a fallacy; it's a false premise.

Why, you may ask?   Because if you don't have an understanding of the—underlying— structures of English, you will end up making sentences, in both speaking and writing, that are confusing, barely understandable or incomprehensible.   As we have repeatedly seen, you will have the tendency to attach English words to Chinese grammar which, in turn, hinders accurate meaning.   Put another way, memorizing long lists of vocabulary will keep you stuck in Chinese English.

Overstressing vocabulary will result in a weak foundation.   By stressing isolated vocabulary items, you are unwittingly impeding your own progress.   You are taking the wrong road; you have a misconception about learning English.   In essence, you are misguided. It's as if you had all the necessary materials to build your home, but not the architectural drawings!   Please believe me, focusing on memorizing vocabulary will leave you high and dry when you reach the shores of an English-speaking country.   Again, it's like building your house on sand.

Kindly consider this all-important question: What use is an extensive vocabulary that stretches from Wuhan to Philadelphia, if you don't have a basic understanding of the vital grammatical structures that holds that vocabulary together?   In other words, what good is an extensive vocabulary, if you don't know how to use the vocabulary correctly in a sentence, let alone in a question?

If you overemphasize vocabulary, if you neglect the grammatical structures of English, you remain "fenced in" a Chinese mindset; there will be no change in your perception, no change in your pattern of thinking, (Please remember that I'm not criticizing the Chinese language or culture.   I'm simply talking about opening our minds to a different way of thinking which language learning requires). Therefore, in all your investigations, make it a priority to focus on grammatical structures, especially those targeted for you, dear student, in this book.   In this way, you will have a solid foundation on which to correctly build your understanding of English, a strong structure on which to—correctly—use new vocabulary.   To do otherwise, I strongly feel, is self-defeating!

Grammatical structures or "You need a cup to hold your tea!"

I repeat: You may "think" that your "problem" is vocabulary, but, in most cases, it isn't.   As we have stated above, vocabulary is important, of course, but is secondary to grammatical structures.   Your "problem" is understanding and using English grammatical structures correctly.   Your "problem," dear student, is having erroneously focused on vocabulary ("what" something means), while neglecting the grammatical structures ("how" it's expressed).

Please keep in mind that VOCABULARY CANNOT STAND ALONE!   IT REQUIRES A STRUCTURE TO HOLD IT IN PLACE, A STRUCTURE TO SUPPORT IT.   In other words, YOU NEED A CUP TO HOLD YOUR TEA!   The cup (the structure) holds the tea (the vocabulary).   Without the cup, your tea will spill all over the table!

In the same way, you need the grammatical structures to hold vocabulary.   Therefore, always put your attention primarily on the grammatical structures.   In spite of appearances to the contrary, ENGLISH—LIKE CHINESE AND ALL OTHER LANGUAGES—IS BASED LARGELY ON ITS GRAMMATICAL STRUCTURES.

The grammatical structures are the very underpinnings of any language.   Understand the structures and you have important keys to English.   It's of the utmost importance that you realize that the grammatical structures, by their very nature, teach you how English "works."   Vocabulary, essentially, doesn't!   The grammatical structures of English provide the necessary support.   They are far more important to your present and future progress than the vocabulary item.

The cup and the tea

Let's take a look at my meaning with a concrete example.   In the simple sentence,

I saw a giraffe,

the grammatical structure of [past tense + article ("saw a")]—which is "the cup"— is far more important to your learning, understanding and progress than the vocabulary item "giraffe"—which is "the tea."   The word "giraffe" can easily be learned and substituted for any other object you may encounter in your everyday life e.g., "a pigeon," "a skyscraper," "a mall," etc.   Thus, "I saw a pigeon," "I saw a skyscraper," etc.   It's the grammatical structure that will ultimately serve you best.   Mastering the grammatical structure will, most likely, require a bit more energy on your part than learning a new word. However, there's a big payoff: 1) you'll be speaking English correctly, 2) native speakers of English will readily understand what you mean and 3) you will be in aligned with what English really is!   Not a bad deal!

You see, dear reader, if you have the correct grammatical structure, all you have to do is "pour in" the new vocabulary item when it comes your way.   In other words, "the cup" will always be in place, ever-ready to receive the new vocabulary, "the tea."   The correct grammatical structure will undoubtedly ensure that you are correctly understood, that your ideas are correctly expressed.   Please keep in mind: THE GRAMMATICAL STRUCTURE FIRST, THEN THE VOCABULARY!   Remember: "YOU NEED A CUP TO HOLD YOUR TEA!"   Again, I ask that you trust me in this.

Beware: the counterproductive practice of *"getting only the general meaning"*

Overemphasizing vocabulary works against you!   Why? Because all your efforts are erroneously aimed at "getting only the general meaning."   What do I mean by this?   Students are inclined to stress isolated vocabulary items, thinking that by doing so, they will "understand" English, i.e., the meaning of the sentence, the paragraph, the essay, etc.   Please believe me when I say that I understand this

"logic," but it's counterproductive.

When you stress vocabulary, you tend to ignore all the

grammatical elements in a sentence that make English, English.

Without realizing it, you are "studying" only a portion of the picture.

As stated above, you tend to emphasize "what" a word means, while

ignoring the other half—the all-important—"how" it's used!   Allow

me to repeat that the "how" contains all the grammatical elements that

make English, English, that gives accurate meaning.   It is crucial to

mastering English.

As a consequence of this false premise of "getting only the

general meaning," students hinder their correct understanding of

English, and, in turn, their progress.   Sadly, they remain stuck in

Chinese English, which, in turn, results in attaching English words to

Chinese grammatical structures!   (Forgive me for stating this yet

again, but I do so because it's crucial to your success).   In doing so,

students end up making sentences like, "Yesterday, I go to class,"

questions like, "You are going to New York?"   I repeat: there will be

little to no expanding of your thinking; you have gained no

understanding of what English really is.   All your efforts have been sacrificed for "getting only the general meaning," a "meaning" that is often vague, unclear or misunderstood!   In essence, you have the wrong view.

How often do students, with markers in hand, highlight in yellow, pink, blue—all the colors of the rainbow—the vocabulary they don't understand, while totally ignoring the essential grammar that holds thoughts—English!—together and gives correct meaning?   Does this sound familiar, dear student?   As mentioned above, this practice is understandable, but counterproductive and self-defeating!   As we say in English, "You are shooting yourself in the foot!"

Please keep in mind that learning English is not a matter of translating individual English words into Chinese.   Remember that English is not a direct translation of Chinese just as Chinese is not a direct translation of English.   Mastering English involves much more than "getting only the general meaning."   Approaching English "to get only the general meaning" will result in retarded progress, while frustrating yourselves, and confusing your English-speaking listeners and readers.   I am convinced that there is no practice more detrimental to your progress than:

1) the faulty practice of overstressing isolated vocabulary,

2) the faulty practice of approaching English "only to get the general meaning."

And yet, it troubles me to say that this is often the average student's main *"technique"* for *"learning"* and *"understanding"* English.

The sentence holds the key

So then, how do you free yourself from this self-defeating focus on isolated vocabulary and "getting only the general meaning" to a more productive, worthwhile, open-ended approach to learning English?   I would strongly encourage you—in all your investigations—to widen your view by focusing on THE ELEMENTS WITHIN A SENTENCE.   Notice that I say THE ELEMENTS WITHIN A SENTENCE, not necessarily the whole sentence. ALWAYS focus on THE ELEMENTS WITHIN A SENTENCE, no matter your level of proficiency.   (Though I use the word "sentence," this idea applies equally to a question).

Why the sentence?   Because the grammatical structures of a language—be it English or Chinese—are always found in the sentence. The sentence contains all the grammatical elements that make English,

English, that make Chinese, Chinese.   THE INDIVIDUAL
SENTENCE HOLDS THE KEY!   As the sentence contains the
grammatical structures of a given language, it readily reveals how
words are used, how they are interconnected, how they change in the
context of a sentence, which, in turn, gives accurate meaning.   The
sentence shows the way a language "thinks," the way a language
"speaks," the way a language "works."   (Isolated vocabulary never
does!) The sentence contains actual, everyday grammar, everyday
language.   We might say that the sentence is where the action is!

     The sentence, if properly approached, will always reveal to you
what you need to know, what you need to work on.   Therefore, make
every effort to focus on the elements within a sentence.   The correct
grammar and meaning are largely in the sentence!   Therefore, avoid
the debilitating practice of burying yourself in lists of vocabulary for
the sole purpose of "getting only the general meaning" of the text.
This is a faulty practice which will, ultimately, not serve you in
mastering English.

The wrong approach vs. the right approach

Allow me to explain what takes place when students read "to get only the general meaning" of the text.   I offer two examples so that you can see the dynamics of this faulty, self-defeating *"learning."*

Example 1: If the average student encounters the English sentence,

He applied to several colleges in the U.S.

he, most likely, will focus—understand—only:

"apply," "several college," "U.S."

Yes, he got "the general meaning," but failed to consider all the important grammatical elements that hold English together, that give accurate meaning.   In essence, he has "converted" English into Chinese!   In other words, HE WAS LOOKING AT ALL THE WRONG THINGS.   Result: he, unfortunately, remains "boxed in," as we have repeatedly noted, in Chinese English.   No progress has been made.   The student has, unwittingly "shot himself in the foot!"

In attempting "to get only the general meaning," he missed, ignored all the important elements that make English, English, all the elements that are teaching him how English "thinks," "speaks," "works."   He overlooked, "<u>He</u>," "app**lied to**," "college**s**," "**in the**

U.S."   These underlined areas are exactly what I mean, dear student, by THE ELEMENTS WITHIN A SENTENCE.

Therefore, may I suggest that you widen your view, that you extend the length of your magic marker line to include:

1)   the word just before and after the nouns and verbs, while

2)   zeroing in on how the nouns and verbs change form in the context of a sentence?

In other words, pay attention to how words relate to each other, how they are linked.   Please don't make the self-defeating mistake of focusing on just the meaning of individual, isolated nouns and verbs, deceiving yourself into thinking that you understand, that you are getting the meaning.

For example, use those magic markers to highlight features such as college**s**, appl**ied to, in the** U.S., etc.   These features, without a doubt, hold the key to understanding and mastering English.   This perspective of widening your focus, of widening the length of your magic marker line will help to free you from Chinese English.   It will, undoubtedly, put you in alignment with what English really is.

Example 2: If the average student reads:

They went to the store to buy a quart of milk.

chances are, she will focus—understand—only:

"go," "store," "buy," "quart," "milk"

Yes, she "got the general meaning," but just as we saw in the previous example, failed to consider all the important grammatical elements that hold English together, that give accurate meaning, that are teaching her how English "thinks," "speaks," "works."

I repeat: please pay close attention to the word just before and after the nouns and verbs, e.g., "**the** store," "**a** quart **of**," "**went to,**" while focusing on how verbs and nouns change form in the context of a sentence, e.g., "**went to**."   If you fail to do this, you will, unfortunately, remain stuck, as we have repeatedly said, in Chinese English.   Aim, then, to break this self-defeating habit.

Reminder: not the entire sentence!

Please keep in mind that we are not referring to the whole sentence, but to **THE ELEMENTS WITHIN A SENTENCE, its parts.**   I do not over-exaggerate when I state that these grammatical elements are extremely important to your progress, are extremely important to your mastering English.   Allow me to repeat that when a student focuses on "getting only the general meaning," via isolated vocabulary, he is, in essence, converting English into Chinese which ultimately keeps him "locked into" a Chinese mindset.   Sadly, he has ignored the structures (the English concepts) that do not conform to his native Chinese.   Please note, dear student, that "converting" works efficiently from yuan to dollars, from Centigrade to Fahrenheit, from kilometers to miles, but it does not work efficiently with language; it does not work efficiently from Chinese to English!

Thus, the necessity of freeing yourself from the paralyzing "malpractice" of stressing vocabulary and "getting only the general meaning."   Thus, the necessity of WIDENING YOUR VIEW; the necessity of CHANGING YOUR PERSPECTIVE.   Please know that when I say "change," I am in no way suggesting that you forsake your rich Chinese language and heritage.   Never!   I am merely suggesting that you "expand" your understanding, that you open your mind to a "new," "different" way of thinking and learning so as to include, to embrace this English perspective.   The sentence, dear student, will open the door!

As previously discussed, the concepts outlined in this book are crucial for mastering English as they keep English standing up, they keep English erect.   Without them, English collapses, falls apart.

The benefits

Investigating in this way, you will be learning how to approach English, how to target the important grammatical items.   You'll be putting your attention where it needs to be: on the language itself as you encounter it.   In other words, you will be working on the language as you find it, in the here and now, in your daily investigations, not on broad grammar rules that tend—in my experience—to put a distance between you and living English.   You will be focusing on the grammar areas of English that differ considerably from your native Chinese, i.e., the areas that most need your pinpointed attention.   Most important, you will be freeing yourself from the gross misconception that meaning is principally in isolated vocabulary.   Please keep in mind that vocabulary is only a part of the picture.   Allow me to remind you that grammatical structures (the "how"), by their very nature, give meaning, teach you how English works.   Vocabulary (the "what") almost never does!

Approaching your learning in this way provides yet another major benefit: you will be LEARNING HOW TO LEARN!   This practice will serve you well—as we previously noted—when you are in an English-speaking country as you will be setting a precedent, while at home in China, for successful, constructive lifelong learning.   Please keep in mind that grammatical structures, vocabulary and pronunciation each play a role in language learning.   In other words, English— language—is not just vocabulary.

To your advantage: English always tells the truth

Please bear in mind that English, like all languages, is ALWAYS TELLING YOU THE TRUTH ABOUT ITSELF.   It's ALWAYS telling you how it "speaks."   It's ALWAYS telling you how it "thinks."   It's ALWAYS telling you how it "works."   It's ALWAYS giving you "the right answer."   You have only to pay attention.   English will ALWAYS tell you the truth.   ALWAYS!   It will NEVER lie to you.   NEVER!   English will never tell you: "I have new car."   NEVER!   It will always tell you the truth—loud and clear—"I have **a** new car."   English will never tell you: "She has many good idea."   NEVER!   EVER!   It will always tell you the truth—loud and clear—"She has many good idea**s**."   English will never tell you, "Last weekend, I go New York."   NEVER!   EVER! It will always tell you the truth—loud and clear—"I **went to** New York **last weekend**."

Therefore, use this insight to your advantage, i.e., pay close attention, be alert to how words change according to the context of the sentence, be alert to the word immediately preceding and following the nouns and verbs.   Once again, this practice of paying pinpointed attention applies equally to the advanced student as to the beginner or to intermediate student.   (Please remember the Chinese MD and PhD candidates).

Concept 6

"going to" vs *"will"*

There is a difference!

Many Chinese students erroneously tend to think that all—or most—future action in English requires the word "will."   This is NOT correct; this is a major misconception about English.   This misconception will lead you to expressing a stiff, incorrect sentence like this:

*I **will** go to China on a business trip next month.*

The native speaker, of course, understands the idea of the sentence, but this is not a correct use of English.   The native speaker of English would spontaneously say:

*I'**m going** to China next month on business.*

Please consider this scenario: ask a Chinese ESL student,

*"What **are you going** to do this weekend?"*

and he will—most likely—answer,

*"**I will** study."*

The native speaker of English would answer,

*"I'**m going** to study."*

Please notice the discrepancy between the question and the Chinese student's answer. English asks, "going to;" the ESL student responds, "will." Would you not agree with me, dear student, that this is another instance where the Chinese student has the wrong concept, is not aligned with what English really is?

Please keep in mind that THE CORRECT ANSWER to most questions is usually found IN THE QUESTION ITSELF. This understanding often escapes the student's notice. Consider:

Question: *What are you **going to do?***

Answer: *I'm **going to** study.*

Notice that the kernel of the answer is in the question. The question, we could say, is actually directing you to the correct answer.

Another scenario. Ask a Chinese student,

"What are you going to do over the break?"

and she will—most likely—answer with something like,

"I will go to New York."

Please notice, again, the discrepancy between the question and the student's answer. English asks, "going to;" the ESL student responds, "will." Would you not agree that this is another instance where the Chinese student has the wrong concept, is not in harmony with what English really is?

Please consider carefully the following everyday future thoughts as they would be spontaneously expressed by a native speaker of English:

I'm going to the library after class.

They're going back to China at the end of the semester.

What are you going to do after graduation?

Where in Canada is Pei Lu going to live?

Enxi's going to organize an event on Chinese culture.

Ping told me that her parents are going to England this summer.   (Notice, it is not necessary to say "going to go").

ATTENTION: MOST FUTURE ACTION IN ENGLISH IS EXPRESSED BY "GOING TO," NOT "WILL."   This is an important concept and crucial in speaking English correctly.

When, then, do we use "will?"

At this point, you may well ask, *"When do we use **will***?*"* Excellent question!   Observe carefully the following three situations in which "will" is used:

1) English uses "will" in response to a polite request.   In this case, "will" indicates a determined intent to obey a (polite) request. The following examples should make this point clcar:

Libby: "Call me when you get there." (a polite request)

Tony: "*I will.*" (This is an obedient/polite/determined response to do what is requested: "I **will** do it," i.e., "I **will** call you when I get there.")

Rose: "It's cold out.   Bundle up." (a polite request)

Dick: "*I will.*" (This is an obedient/polite/determined response to do what is requested: "I **will** do it," i.e., "I **will** bundle up.")

Marion: "*Don't forget your keys.*" (a polite request)

Gene: "*I won't.*" (This is an obedient/polite/determined response to do what is requested: "I **won't** do it," i.e., "I **won't** forget my keys.")

Teacher: "*Practice your English.*" (a polite request)

Student: "*I will.*" (This is an obedient/polite/determined response to do what is requested: "I **will** do it," i.e., "I **will** practice my English.")

2) English also uses "will" to answer a remark/a statement that requires an immediate—therefore, future—action/response.   Kindly consider the following examples, carefully.

Sam: "Someone's at the door."

Jennie: "**I'll** get it." (This is an immediate—right away—future action/response).

Diane: "It's hot in here."

Ruth: "**I'll** open the windows." (This is an immediate—right away—future action/response).

Mother: "This chair is heavy!"

Dad: "Wait, **I'll** give you a hand." (This is an immediate—right away—future action/response).

Joanne: "That light bulb just blew out."

Ron: "Hang on, **I'll** change it." (This is an immediate—right away—future action/response).

3) English, additionally, uses "will" in a two-clause sentence where one of the clauses expresses a condition that begins with "if." Observe in following examples how the future clause of the sentence ("will") depends upon a condition in the "if" clause:

If I have the time, "I'll go to the library.

If it rains, they'll take a cab.

She'll stay in this country after graduation, if she finds a job.

Please note, as in this last example, that it doesn't matter whether the **if-clause** is in the first or second position.   The idea can be expressed either way.

Please remember that although the above three situations use "will," future action in everyday, standard English is usually expressed by "going to."   This is another essential concept of English where Chinese students are often out of alignment.   Now that you know the difference, I hope you're **going to** use it correctly.

Concept 7

The impersonal "you"

A major oversight

Even the most advanced Chinese students of English are usually unaware of the impersonal "you" or are hesitant to use it. This oversight comes, once again, from their—quite understandable, but incorrect—tendency to translate their thoughts, word-for-word, from Chinese into English.

Consequently, the correct English does not feel "right" to them. Please remember that English is not a translation of Chinese, just as Chinese is not a translation of English. I continue to stress this fundamental concept of language learning because most students do not have this essential awareness, yet, it's all-important in mastering English.

Students are prone to assume that if it makes sense in Chinese then, it must make sense in English! Again, nothing could be farther from the truth. (If you approach English as a direct translation of Chinese, you, most certainly, do not have the right view). Therefore, please keep in mind that English does not "think" like Chinese, that

English does not "speak" like Chinese, that English is not a translation of Chinese.   Please understand, dear student, this is not a cultural bias; it's a simple neutral fact!

Not "you" in particular, but "people" in general

So, let's investigate how the impersonal "you" is overlooked— and mistakenly expressed—by native speakers of Chinese.   Here are a few examples.

Example 1: Chinese students will, invariably, ask,

"How to spell?"

(Please take a moment now and question yourself.   Is this not the way you express the question in Chinese?   Is this not Chinese grammar with English words?)   English, however, says,

"How do you spell it?"

The "you" in this question is impersonal; it doesn't mean your listener.   It means "people," in general.   In other words, "How do people spell it?"   This everyday English question reflects how English "thinks," how English "speaks."

Example 2: Chinese students will invariably ask,

"How to say?"

(Please take a moment again and question yourself.   Is this not the way you express the question in Chinese?   Is this not Chinese grammar with English words?)   English, however, says,

"How do you say it?"

The "you" is impersonal; it doesn't mean your listener.   It means "people" in general.   In other words, "How do people say it?" Again, this everyday English question reflects how English "thinks," how English "speaks."

Example 3: Chinese students will invariably ask,

"How to pronounce?"

(Again, I ask that you please take a moment now and question yourself.   Is this not the way you express the question in Chinese?   Is this not Chinese grammar with English words?)   English, however, says—and I hope that the pattern has now become obvious to you—

"How do you pronounce it?"

The "you" is impersonal; it doesn't mean your listener.   It means "a person in general."   In other words, "How do people pronounce it?"   As with the above two examples, this everyday English question reflects how English "thinks," how English "speaks.

The impersonal "you" in sentences

The impersonal "you" is also used in sentences.   Again, the "you" in the sentence is not your listener, but is a general statement implying "people" in general.   Here are some examples of how the impersonal "you" would be used in everyday American English:

Example 1:

To be good parents, you have to have understanding.

(In other words, "To be good parents, people have to have understanding.")

Example 2:

You should always be considerate of others.

(In other words, "People should always be considerate of others.")

Example 3:

You should be careful when crossing a busy street.

(In other words, "People should always be careful when crossing a busy street.")

Example 4:

To have a friend, you have to be a friend.

(In other words, "To have a friend, people have to be a friend.")

Example 5:

You have to love life, if you're going to enjoy life.

(In other words, "People have to love life, if people are going to enjoy life.")

In each of the above sentences, "you" is impersonal; IT DOESN'T MEAN YOUR LISTENER.   It means "people" in general. I find that Chinese students tend to shy away from using the impersonal "you," erroneously thinking they are directly addressing their listener(s).   Let me assure you that the native speaker of English will understand your meaning and will interpret your thought correctly.

A word to the wise! 2

I can assure you that mastering the impersonal "you" will help you immensely in gaining an "entry" into how English "thinks." Doors will begin to fly open for you.   You will be stepping into the very atmosphere of English.   It will help you to gain the correct perspective on English.   It will open your mind, it will align you to what English really is.

Concept 8

The "Maybe" Syndrome & the Importance of Careful Listening

Maybe, maybe, maybe!

Chinese ESL students tend to punctuate every spoken sentence with the word "maybe." Here are a few actual student remarks:

He's coming tomorrow, maybe.

I can do it, maybe.

Maybe, the professor will understand.

Maybe, I don't know the word.

I think maybe my English needs improvement.

Ask a Chinese student,

"Are you going to the party this weekend?"

and he, most likely, will answer, *"Maybe."* This repeated use of *"maybe"* is not an English way of speaking. It is actually Chinese English. As you know, English definitely has the word *"maybe"* and, yes, we definitely use it, but we don't use it as frequently as Chinese does.

Following are a few examples of how American English expresses the idea of *"maybe"* in everyday thought, in everyday conversation.   Please consider them carefully as they will show you a great deal about how English "thinks," how English "speaks."   They will hclp you to gain an added "entry" into what English really is. They will reveal that language learning involves CAREFUL LISTENING, CHANGING YOUR VIEW AND EXPANDING YOUR WAY OF THINKING.

Below are possible responses in everyday English to the question, *"Are you going to the party this weekend?"*   Each example expresses an English way of saying "maybe."

"I think so."

"I might."

"I'm thinking about it."

"I haven't decided yet."

All these responses express uncertainty, and are the usual forms of expressing *"maybe"* in everyday English conversation.

English also expresses *"maybe"* by using an *"if-clause."* Thus, possible responses to *"Are you going to the party this weekend?"* might be:

"If I get my homework done."

"If I have the time."

"If my boyfriend wants to."

"If I can get a ride."

Listening carefully is a vital component of successful language learning.

What does this overuse of *"maybe"* by Chinese students show us?   What can we learn from it?   Basically—I feel—it shows us, once again, that the student falsely thinks that English is a direct translation of Chinese, and thus translates word-for-word from his native Chinese to English.   Additionally, and of equal importance, it shows us that the student is not listening to the new language; he's listening principally to his internal dialogue in his native Chinese. This, of course, is understandable and "natural," particularly for beginners.

However, the intermediate and advanced student should begin to attune himself to English by listening more carefully to what is actually being said in the English-speaking environment.   Failure to do so will unwittingly keep you stuck in Chinese English, a.k.a., Chinglish.   Our aim, then, is to help free you from a limiting mindset.

Therefore, in all your interactions with native speakers—whether in person, or via the Internet—listen carefully, keep your ears open.

If you are listening carefully, you'll begin to hear, for example, that native speakers of English are not regularly repeating *"maybe."* Conversely, you will discover that you are!   If you are listening carefully, you'll begin to hear, to notice what native speakers repeatedly say in their everyday conversation.

You will hear again and again, for examp*le, "I might," "Yes, I did," "I guess," "Wouldn't you?," "it seems," "No, you shouldn't," "more or less," "got it?," "kind of,"* etc.   Make a habit of listening for these repeated utterances; they will help tremendously in putting you in alignment with everyday English.

As with reading, students tend to listen only to comprehend the gist of what is being said.   Again, this is understandable. Nonetheless, attempt to open your ears, to be attentive to what native speakers are actually saying, no matter your level of learning.

Insights into Successful Learning 5

Take advantage of the opportunity

Developing good listening skills depends primarily, in large part, on participating in the English-speaking world. Studying from your textbook is not enough! Being in an American classroom—whether it's English or history—is not enough.

I understand that it's only natural to spend your free time with your Chinese friends, speaking Chinese. Believe me, I know what it's like! I remember my own experiences in Spain and Latin America, finding it much easier to be with my American and British friends than venturing forth into the Spanish-speaking world. However, I came to realize that I would never learn Spanish by speaking English. The same holds true for you: you'll never learn English by speaking Chinese! Therefore, it's absolutely essential for your progress and success to place yourself—as much as you can—in the English-speaking environment.

Trust me when I tell you that Chinese students who live with American families and/or who spend their free time participating with Americans in American life make far greater progress than those who—forgive me—huddle together with their Chinese friends, speaking Chinese. The difference in their English proficiency is immediately noticeable; they are more at ease with English and with American life. Therefore, dear student, if you have the opportunity of a homestay, TAKE IT! If you have the opportunity to room with American classmates, TAKE IT! These are golden opportunities which will help your English to soar.

Please keep in mind that hearing English on a regular basis is as important as speaking it. These skills go hand-in-hand. Consequently, I strongly suggest that you make every effort to participate in the everyday life of the English-speaking country where you decide to study. I know it's not always easy, but it's doable and essential for your success.

Remember: the more time you spend with English-speaking people, the more your English will improve; the more your English improves, the easier it becomes to speak and understand. In other words, you will grow in your language skills and, equally important, in self-confidence.

Another major misconception

Not long ago, I stressed to a Chinese student the importance of improving her English.   She responded that she didn't have the time nor the money to take classes.   Taking classes was the farthest thing from my mind!   (Here was a breakdown in communication for which I take full responsibility).   I was thinking that she could improve her English by participating more actively in everyday American life, i.e., use her English, immerse herself in living English; thereby, making progress.   (Please recall the above discussion about Chinese students who live with American families and the progress they make).   She, on the other hand, was thinking classes!   I was thinking, "play the piano," she was thinking, "learn about the piano."

I cite this example because it reveals the mistaken attitude—the misconception—that many Chinese students have.   They, like this student, see their improvement as being dependent on classes, but, in fact, their progress is dependent on using English, participating in everyday American life.   Their situation is, to me, like a man dying of thirst, but not realizing that he's in a freshwater lake!   Please keep in mind that the more you immerse yourself in living English, the clearer it will become to you, the better progress you will make.   Please remember, dear student, that all true learning is in life.   Life is the teacher.

For the timid student: Dad's advice

When I was in high school, my Father saw that I was timid, often afraid to try new things.   He offered me this life-changing advice which I now share with you.   He said, "When you are afraid to do something in life, do it anyway, don't be afraid, because in 5-years time, you'll look back and realize, you'll see clearly that there was nothing to be afraid of."   He was right!   Excellent advice which has served me all my life.   I sincerely hope it will serve you, too!

So, if you feel shy about entering an English-speaking environment, remember my Father's advice because, at some point in the future, you'll look back and realize that you had been foolish, that there had been nothing to be afraid of!

A worthwhile use of technology

Whether you are reading this in China, or are actually living in an English-speaking country at this time, you can easily get into the habit of listening carefully by taking advantage of technology.   In this day and age, dear student, you have ready-access, 24/7, to hear—and see—everyday English in a wide variety of formats.   Following are two examples of constructive ways to use technology.

Example 1: You might watch a minute or two of an American news broadcast, an ad or a posting on, say, *YouTube.*   Play it two or three times, jotting down any words or phrases that you readily understand. (There is no harm in repeated listenings as each time the English will become clearer and clearer to you).   Then, play it again, sentence by sentence, pausing between sentences to write down what you have understood.   Proceed in this fashion until the end of the one or two-minute segment.   Repeat this procedure as many times as you see fit, i.e., until you feel that you have transcribed most of the news broadcast or ad.

This type of exercise will provide you with an opportunity to encounter English that is alive!   It's an excellent way to put yourself in an English-speaking environment no matter where you are!   In essence, you'll be learning how to listen, you'll be learning how to learn!   You'll be attuning yourself to everyday English.   Whether you are in China or living abroad, this practice will put you at an advantage; it will immerse you in a living English environment.

Imagine how carefully you will have to listen when practicing in this way.   This practice will put you in touch with what English really is. (You might find this exercise even more beneficial and fun, if you do it with one or two of your friends.   You might find it even more beneficial and fun, if you followed the above procedure while listening to your favorite American or British singers with your friends!)

Example 2: You could watch a Chinese movie on the Internet with English subtitles.   Hearing the Chinese and reading the English subtitles, you will easily learn how English expresses itself.   You, more than likely, will have many *"aha"* experiences.   You will find yourself exclaiming, *"Aha, that's how you express that idea in English!"* (I, myself, used this technique while living in Spain and Latin America and learned a great deal.   I, however, could only use it at the movies!)

Please keep in mind that it really doesn't matter if you don't catch every single word in a movie, ad, or song.   What is important is that you are listening to everyday English, that you are immersing yourself in English.   Believe me when I say that it's of major importance that you hear English, that you listen to it.   Listen to it, even if you don't understand!   The above exercises will provide you with an entry into everyday spoken English.   As previously discussed, these practices have the advantage of familiarizing you with English that is used repeatedly ("kind of," "more or less," "I think," "just in case," "it seems to me," etc.)   If you don't listen, you remain in a vacuum, hearing only yourself which virtually means hearing only Chinese English.   (Remember, *"maybe," "maybe," "maybe."*)   And, don't leave it at listening alone.   Begin to use these frequently repeatedly expressions when you are speaking English, i.e., put them into use immediately.   They will give you an increased feeling of self-confidence, an increased feeling of mastering English.

Modern technology affords you opportunity after opportunity to hear English, to participate actively in the English-speaking world. Your parents and your grandparents did not have this opportunity.   Be smart, dear student, and use it to your highest advantage!

The *"aha"* of the real-life situation

The real-life situation—whether by living in the host country or via technology—is often key to your progress, to your understanding. You will be amazed to discover that what was once a mystery to you on the written page will become clear when heard and experienced in a real-life situation.

You will be amazed to discover that an English sentence or expression that you were unable to understand in a book—even though you understood every single word—will become crystal clear in real-life situations.   You will hit your forehead and say to yourself, *"Aha, now I understand!"*   **Please keep in mind that a real-life situation often gives more meaning than the words themselves!**   So, as suggested above, be sure to put yourself in the everyday life of English! This point cannot be overemphasized.   I can assure you that your English will improve by leaps and bounds.   Time spent interacting with native speakers of English will yield far greater improvement than hours spent sequestered in your room studying English in a book! Again, I ask that you trust me in this matter.

I, myself, have had many experiences when learning Spanish where I understood every word in a written phrase, but the meaning escaped me.   Once in a Spanish-speaking world, hearing the phrase in a particular situation, the meaning—much to my joy—immediately became clear to me.   *"Aha, I got it!" "I now know what they mean!"* The real-life situation "explained" the meaning to me.   Please keep in mind that a situation often gives more meaning than the words themselves!

A word to the wise! 3

Let me stress, however, that you use technology wisely. Technology can be very seductive. We want to use it with good judgment. We want to be careful that we understand who is the "master" and who is the "slave." What may initially seem harmless fun, may evolve into a destructive addiction. No matter how colorful, how active, how exciting technology may appear to be, human-to-human interaction is always, by far, the richer, more rewarding experience. People—life—should always come first, always! Please do not lose sight of this, no matter what your age, no matter what you are doing, or with whom you are doing it, HUMAN MEETING HUMAN always takes precedence.

Practice thinking in English!

THINKING IN ENGLISH is another technique that will greatly help you to make good progress. I would suggest that you spend a certain amount of time each day thinking ONLY in English. Begin with a time limit of, say, just five minutes and gradually—at your own discretion—increase the length of time.   The only stipulation is that you spend the allotted time THINKING ONLY IN ENGLISH, forming all your ideas in English.   This simple, but effective, exercise will require you—by its very nature—to reflect on what you are attempting to express.   It will require you to become increasingly aware of how to use English correctly.   In the silence of your own mind—unhampered by social pressure—you will begin to question yourself about the accuracy of your English.

If, during the time of your "English thinking," you hit a block or a doubt—a place where you don't know how to express your particular idea in English, i.e., you don't know how to finish your thought—then, jot it down and, at an appropriate time, ask your teacher, or discuss it with a classmate(s).

I, myself, used this technique of thinking in Spanish when I was living in Spain and Latin America.   (I still do!)   I would think my everyday thoughts in Spanish—while on the bus, for example, or walking down the street—as we all naturally do in our mother tongue in our everyday lives.

When I came to a thought that I couldn't finish or had serious doubts about its accuracy, I would jot it down and—when the opportunity presented itself—question a native Spanish-speaking friend.   It might be something such as:

"Do you say, 'He went to Italy for studying Italian,' "

or do you say

"He went to Italy to study Italian."

What a relief—and joy—it was to discover that

"He went to Italy to study Italian"

was the correct way to say it.   This practice had the added advantage of improving my understanding as I would tend to recognize the grammatical point in question whenever I heard it.   *"Ah, yes, there it is again, I would say to myself, 'She went downtown to do her Christmas shopping.' "*   Different idea, but the same structure! Hurray!   I'm learning!

Concept 9

"even though" vs *"even"*

They look similar, but they aren't.

In English, "even though" and "even" have two different, distinct meanings.   They are not the same!   They look similar, but they aren't.   Chinese students of English are inclined not to distinguish between them.   They are likely to use only "even."   In other words, they tend to say and write "even" in sentences that require "even though."   Additionally, in spite of understanding the correct meaning of "even," they misplace it in an English sentence.   Let's investigate!

Contrasting "even though" and "even"

To help you better understand, to make the matter clear, I have indicated the Chinese English on the left and the correct English on the right.   As previously noted, contrast—like its friend "mistake"—is an excellent learning technique.   Contrast, by its very nature, helps you to gain awareness, to pinpoint the mistake and to correct it.   Allow me to emphasize that contrast creates a bridge for you to move from where you are to where you want to be. The learning technique of contrast allows for continuity and progress; it frees you. Result: correct understanding, relief, progress and joy!

Chinese English	English
Even *he had homework to do, he went out with his friends.*	**Even though** *he had homework to do, he went out with his friends.*
Even *she has a car, she takes the train to work.*	**Even though** *she has a car, she takes the train to work.*
Even *they've lived in the U.S. for many years, they don't speak English.*	**Even though** *they've lived in the U.S. for many years, they don't speak English.*
Even *they weren't stylish, the phones were like well-trained workers.*	**Even though** *they weren't stylish, the phones were like well-trained workers.*
Even *he was sometimes erratic, they were willing to work for him.*	**Even though** *he was sometimes erratic, they were willing to work for him.*

Notice that in all the above sentences—both in Chinese English and English—there is a result that is contrary to reason, contrary to logic; a result that is opposite to what is expected (**She takes the train to work,** a situation that is contrary to what is expected because **she has a car!**). In such situations where there is a result that is opposite to what is expected, English says "even though."

A dynamic trio

To help you gain a better understanding of when to use "even though," keep in mind that "although" is a synonym for "even though." Take, for example, the above sentence,

Even though he had homework to do, he went out with his friends.

If we substitute "although" for "even though," we discover that

Although he had homework to do, he went out with his friends,

has exactly the same meaning!   This practice, this awareness that "even though" and "although" are synonyms will surely guide you to use "even though" correctly.

To deepen your understanding of "even though," keep in mind that "in spite of" is yet another synonym for "even though."   Consider the above example of

Even though she has a car, she takes the train to work.

If we substitute "in spite of" for "even though" we discover that

In spite of having a car, she takes the train to work.

has exactly the same meaning!   Notice, however, the change in the verb: in spite of "hav**ing**."   "in spite of" will always required the *-ing* form of the verb.   Thus, English says "in spite of do**ing**," "in spite of go**ing**," "in spite of com**ing**," etc.

May I suggest that you take a look at the above examples of "even though" and change them to a sentence, first with "although" and then with "in spite of."   Interchanging "although" and "in spite of" with "even though" will, once again, help you to have a clearer understanding of using "even though" correctly.   It will help you tremendously in getting a better handle on this grammatical point. What's more, it will show you that language—English—is flexible.

Take notice that the concept of "even though" is the same in both Chinese and English, but is expressed differently.   Chinese, it seems, expresses the idea by using only **"even."**   In English, however, it's necessary to express the idea by using "even though. "   Keep in mind that in situations where the result is the opposite of what you expected, English says, "even though" as in

Even though he is on a diet, he ordered French fries.

"even," investigated

Now that you have an awareness—an entry—into the meaning and use of "even though," it should be easier for you to use "even" correctly in English, especially since you use it similarly in Chinese. THE ONLY DIFFERENCE BEING IN ITS PLACEMENT IN A SENTENCE.   Let's investigate the sentences below to clarify the matter.   (Again, contrast is a valuable, constructive technique in learning).

First, take a careful look at the Chinese English sentence on the left.   Observe it carefully.   Then, look at the English sentence on the right.

Chinese English	English
Even *he doesn't know their address.*	*He doesn't **even** know their address.*
Even she can't remember his name.	*She can't **even** remember his name.*
Even *they don't have time to cook their own dinner.*	*They don't **even** have time to cook own dinner.*
Even *they don't care.*	*They don't **even** care.*
Even *I don't want to think about it.*	*I don't **even** want to think about it.*

What difference do you immediately see?   Yes, you're right, the position of the word "even."   Where is "even" in the Chinese sentence?   Yes, at the beginning.   Where is it in the English sentence?   Yes, before the action word/the verb.   This is a considerable difference and extremely important!   The meaning in both languages is the same, but the placement of the word "even" differs significantly.

Let me point out, dear student, that this is the kind of investigation you should be doing in all your learning, i.e., look, observe, think for yourself.   Allow me also to point out that the placement of "even" in the Chinese English sentence makes the sentence awkward, confusing in English.   It gives the impression that the student doesn't speak English well.   What's more, it may cause confusion for your listener.

Practicing "even though" and "even"

In the way of an exercise, you might write five sentences with "even though" and five sentences with "even."   In so doing, you will give yourself the opportunity to work out your confusion until you hit upon the correct understanding.

This exercise would be particularly effective if done with a friend.   If you have doubts, ask your teacher.   I'm sure he will enthusiastically welcome your interest.

Flashing Yellow Light.

As with all the concepts in this book, "even though" and "even" will require you to change your pattern of thinking.   You are used to the Chinese pattern.   Now English is asking you to change, to expand your way of thinking, to align yourself with its way of thinking.   I assure you that you can do it.   It will, however, require your awareness, followed by regular, meaningful practice.

Insights into Successful Learning 6

"A suit of armor"

In all your investigations, be careful not to become bogged down by grammar rules. Think of rules as guidelines. They are NOT necessarily, as we say in English, "etched in stone."

Although well-intended, classroom instruction—with its overemphasis on rules—tends to put students in what I call, "a grammar-rule suit of armor." What do I mean by this? When grammar rules are overstressed, students become cut off from the life of English; they become isolated from what English really is. They acquire a mistaken idea—a misconception—about English. They are inclined to view English as static, as an "academic subject," which, in my view, it is not. (Kindly remember our discussion of the piano lesson). Sadly, students erroneously view English as fixed, unbending structures. (Please keep in mind that English is *alive*, is flexible and has a "feel"!) As a result of this stress on rigid rules, their spoken and written English can tend to be mechanical, stiff, robot-like. In other words, their English doesn't flow; it doesn't breathe. It's as if they—and English—were in a suit of armor, neither one able to move freely.

The consequences

In this state of mind, students are apt to dismiss—or be frustrated by—whatever doesn't conform to their rule-dominated mindset.   They may unconsciously reject "the unexpected," "the new," that they encounter on their learning path, instead of attempting to integrate it into their understanding, instead of expanding their way of thinking.

I often encounter students who are so restricted by grammar rules that they cannot express themselves freely.   They are so constrained by rigid rules that they cannot "hear" or "feel" the language when in an English-speaking environment.   It's as if they had a textbook in front of their eyes and a textbook over each ear, blocking them from being in direct contact with living English.

Therefore, let all your investigations be free from the rigidity of rote learning, let your investigations be lighthearted, geared toward being open to the "unexpected" that you encounter.   Maintaining this open-minded attitude will help you to see that the rules are like road signs, showing you a direction.

Inconsistencies

If you maintain this open-minded attitude, you will be better equipped to meet the inconsistencies that you meet along your way to mastering English.   Allow me to share with you an important lesson that I learned from a master teacher.

In an Italian class, we were struggling with—and resisting—an inconsistency in Italian that we had newly encountered.   Like most students, we had learned the "rules;" we had become familiar with certain patterns and, unrealistically, expected all of Italian to conform to them.   Our astute teacher—a native speaker of Italian—seeing our frustration, simply said to us in English, *"I'm sorry, but I didn't invent the language; that's just the way it is!"*   I almost fell off my chair! What an insight!   What a relief!

This simple remark lifted a heavy burden from our shoulders and I hope it does the same for you.   It freed us from expecting what was, in essence, unrealistic.   It felt as if a door had opened within me and fresh air was now flowing through; it helped to remove the suit of armor that I didn't know I was wearing.   Inconsistencies were no longer a block.   I saw that it was unrealistic to think that any language—like life itself, like individuals themselves—would be 100% consistent!   Impossible!

Maintaining an open mind

This open attitude toward inconsistencies in English helps to free us from the chains of too much rule-dominated learning that often misguides us, giving us the wrong impression, and which ultimately gets in the way of our learning, our progress.   Maintaining an open mind frees us from the misconception—the unrealistic expectation— that every aspect of a language must conform to the rules that we have, mistakenly—often, slavishly—over-invested in.   This perspective allows us to open up to the new language as we find it, thereby facilitating our learning.   It helps us to shed preconceived—often rigid—ideas.   In short, it teaches us to be flexible.   This open-minded, more relaxed attitude is crucial in all your learning.   It's akin to the attitude we had when learning our mother tongue; we did not fuss over inconsistencies.

How children learn; how we learned

Allow me to illustrate.   (Though I simplify the issue, the essence of it is true).   When American children, for example, encounter an inconsistency in learning English, they don't ask, *"Why, mother?"*; they don't challenge the adults around them with *"This doesn't follow the rule!"*   They simply accept it and move on.   When American parents, for instance, correct their children for saying "he brung" instead of "he brought," the children don't argue the point; they accept it and move on.   (It may take a few corrections, but it will eventually become integrated into the child's understanding).   This, no doubt, happens in Chinese as well.   It happens no matter what our native language.   So let us keep this attitude alive in ourselves when learning English.   I am in no way suggesting that you shouldn't ask questions when in doubt.   You know me well enough by now to know that I am the last teacher on the face of the earth to discourage asking questions.   I am, however, suggesting that, AT TIMES, it's simply more efficacious to accept.   Attempt to see the difference.   As previously mentioned, let your investigations be lighthearted, geared toward being open to *"the unexpected,"* *"the unfamiliar"* that you meet on your path of learning English.

Concept 10

Prepositions: Little Words With S-o-o-o Much Meaning!

The B-I-G role of little prepositions

Whenever I indicate to students that a sentence requires a preposition, they are usually at a loss.   (Please forgive me, but they are).   They look at me bewildered!   At best, they may feebly offer "of " or "on" or "to" but that's it.   No more!   How could this be, I ask myself?   Take a look, dear student, at a printed page of English and you will be amazed to see how often prepositions occur.   (In fact, I would invite you—this very minute—to take a look at any page of printed English and underline or highlight every preposition.   You will readily see what I mean).   Yet, the average student will tend to skim right over them as if they didn't exist, as if they were unimportant, as if they have no meaning!   Again, this is—it seems to me—the result of students over-stressing 1) "getting only the general meaning," 2) of not paying attention to how English expresses itself.

In other words, students tend to zero in on only the verb, while neglecting to pay attention to the all-important little word—the preposition—that immediately follows it. YOU PAY A HEAVY PRICE, DEAR STUDENT, FOR THIS FAULTY VIEW, FOR THIS FAULTY PREMISE.

As we have previously stated, this is understandable, but it's self-defeating. In attempting "to get only the general meaning," you remain stuck in Chinese English. Since prepositions play a vital role in English, please don't dismiss their importance, please don't overlook them. Since they play an integral role in English, it behooves you to consider their significance, to widen your view, to acknowledge their importance in mastering English. Like "The 4 Golden Keys," they will put you in alignment with what English really is.

Verbs and prepositions

With this in mind, let's investigate, look at how prepositions function in English as regards:

1) "2-word verbs,"

2) expressing the whole verb.

1) "2-word verbs"

Nowadays, many grammar books use the term "phrasal verb" for what used to be called "2-word verbs." Sadly, "phrasal verb" means little to the average ESL student. (I would venture to say that the same holds true for the average native speaker of English!). "Phrasal verbs" is not, in my experience, a user-friendly term. On the other hand, "a 2-word verb" goes directly to the heart of the matter. It's a down-to-earth term that says—exactly—what it is. Result: clarity, no confusion. Walt Whitman's wisdom, I feel, is applicable here:

Nothing is better than simplicity.

The verbs in question have 2 parts—yes, sometimes, 3 as in the case of "to make up for," "to catch up with," "to hold on to,"—but generally 2, so the term "2-word verb"—I feel—is clear, to the point, less misleading for you, the student and, therefore, best serves your purpose.

As though it were ONE word

Students often have difficulty with "2-word verbs" because they tend to approach them as two separate words, which, of course, is understandable.   Their mistake, however, is to focus solely on the first word (the verb/the action word which they mistakenly see as the only important word).   In doing so, they neglect to give equal attention to the second little word (the preposition, which, in fact, is of equal importance, but which they see as unimportant).   The truth, dear student, is that both words comprise the verb, not just the first word! In other words, THEY ARE 2 WORDS, BUT 1 VERB; 2 WORDS, BUT 1 IDEA.

Therefore, I would strongly recommend that you reconsider your perspective and look at these quintessentially English verbs AS THOUGH THEY WERE ONE WORD, NOT TWO.   I know that this may sound counterintuitive, but it isn't.

Wait a minute, please!

At this moment, you are most likely thinking, "Wait a minute, Prof. Little!" "You say to look at them as though they were 1 word, but they are, in fact, 2 words?"   "Anyone can see that."   Yes, dear student, you're absolutely right, but from an English perspective, they are 1 verb.   Your task, then, is to change your thinking and to begin to see them as native speakers of English do: **1 verb, 1 idea.**   Let's take a

look at their correct pronunciation as it will help you to better
understand them as 1 verb.   Bear with me as I explain.

How it works.

In everyday English, "2-word verbs" are NOT pronounced as 2
separate, individual words, but as 1, 2-syllable word.   Let's
investigate!

Let's take as our example, "the 2-word verb," "wake up."
Now, please watch and listen carefully to see what happens:
When the last consonant sound of the verb—in our example [k] of
"wake"—meets with the first vowel sound of—in our case [ʌ] of "up"—
we say, "wa-kup."   "wake up" is then pronounced like 1 word of 2
syllables.   This tying together of sounds, this 'linking" of sounds, is
called "liaison."   Thus, pronunciation supports our view that "2-word
verbs" are essentially like 1 word, that they form 1 verb.

A little experiment, right now

Example 1:

Please take a moment now and say aloud "the 2-word verb"
"turn on" as 2 separate words (as you are inclined to do).   Fine!

Now, say them as 1 word with 2 syllables: "tur-non". Do you see my point, or should I say, "Do you hear my point?" Their pronunciation—their sound—is very different. That's because liaison ties them together, making them like 1 word, 1 verb.

Example 2:

Say, "log out" as 2 separate words (as you usually do). Then, say, "lo-gout" as 1 word with 2 syllables. Again, do you see my point, do you hear my point? Their pronunciation—their sound—is very different. That's because liaison, as we have just seen, links them together, making them like 1 word, 1 idea, 1 verb.

Example 3:

Say, "look up," as 2 separate words (as you usually do), then, say "loo-kup" as 1 word with 2 syllables. Again, do you see my point, do you hear my point? Their pronunciation—their sound—is very different. Liaison combines them, making them, in essence, like 1 word, 1 verb.

So, you see, dear student, if you're thinking "log + on," and the native speaker of English is saying, "lo-gon," you will be at a disadvantage because you will not readily understand what is being said. You will be out of alignment with spoken English. (Also, please keep in mind that your native speaker will more readily understand you, if you say "lo-gon!")

Doesn't it then make sense then to adjust your perspective and begin to view these "2-word verbs"—these quintessentially English verbs—as though they were 1 verb, 1 idea in both meaning and pronunciation, because, in fact, they are?   This correct pronunciation reinforces the idea that these seemingly 2 distinct words are, fundamentally, like 1 word, 1 verb.

Focusing on this pronunciation will help your spoken English to flow like a native speaker's; it will help remove the often-present "staccato"/choppiness from your spoken English.   (ESL students tend to speak each word separately, each word disconnected from the next. Native speakers, no matter what the language, never do!).   Practicing this pronunciation will put you in harmony with the language as it's actually spoken in the English-speaking world.   Again, it will align you with what English really is!

Practicing the "liaisons" of "2-word verbs"

Begin by repeating—aloud—the 5 examples below, listening carefully to yourself as you repeat each one.   Remember that the final consonant sound of the first word "links" with, "connects" with the initial vowel sound of the second word.   Repeat them again and again until they begin to feel natural to you

> *English says, "tur-noff," not "turn   off"*
>
> *English says, "co-min," not "come   in"*
>
> *English says, "pi-ckup," not "pick   up"*
>
> *English says, "cli-ckon," not "click   on"*
>
> *English says, "loo-kout," not "look   out"*

Once you feel confident with these above examples, write your own examples of 2-word verbs, say 4 to 6, the more the better.   Then, practice your examples aloud.   It might be something like this:

> *English says, "stan-dup," not "stand up"*
>
> *English says, "tur-non," not "turn on"*
>
> *English says, "kee-pon," not "keep on."*
>
> *English says, "fin-dout," not "find out"*
>
> *English says, "che-ckout," not "check out"*

Again, repeat them again and again until they feel natural to you.   As we've indicated previously, this type of exercise would be very effective if you practiced it with a friend.   It would give you both the opportunity to pronounce, to listen to and to become accustomed to the sound of these uniquely English verbs, not to mention the opportunity to correct each other!

This exercise could be expanded by making a short, spontaneous sentence or question— aloud—with "the 2-word verbs" you have practiced above.   For example, you could say, *"Tur-non the lights, please"* or *"Che-ckout their website."*

And, don't forget our discussion about using technology constructively.   While writing down a 2-minute ad, or when watching a movie, listen carefully for liaisons because I can assure, dear student, they will be there!

By doing this, you will discover that your learning is effective and enjoyable.   The awareness of liaison—followed by regular practice—will put you in tune with English; it will harmonize you to the music of English.   Result: improved understanding for you and for your listener by actually playing the piano!   **(Please keep in mind that "liaison" will occur with the majority of "2-word verbs").**

An added benefit

If you pronounce "2-word verbs" as 1 word, you will avoid a common pronunciation error that students often make.   Consider this, please: if you pronounce "take out" as 2 separate words, you, most likely, will say "ta ou," dropping the [k] and [t] sound.   "Why does this happen?"

As we have seen in our discussion of plurals, this "dropping" of the final consonant sound in English occurs because the Chinese language doesn't have consonant sounds—or strong consonant sounds—at the end of its words.   Consequently, native Chinese speakers, unconsciously, transfer this pattern to English.   Therefore, "take" becomes "ta," "name" becomes "na" etc.

However, if you learn "take out" as 1 word with 2 syllables, acknowledging the liaison that exists between "take" and "out," you will pronounce the verb correctly, thereby, avoiding dropping the final consonant sound!   You will correctly say, "ta-kout," not "ta-ou".   By practicing in this way, you will become increasingly accustomed to pronouncing final consonant sounds, and, thus, more likely to apply it to all final consonants you encounter on your journey of mastering English, saying, for example, "ou[t], and not "ou."   Not a bad deal, right?

Bringing it closer to home

To increase your understanding of liaisons, listen for them in everyday spoken Chinese.   Yes, Chinese, yours as well as your friends' and family's.   Listen for them on TV or in the movies. Listen for them because they're there.   You will be amazed to discover how frequently they occur in your native Chinese.

I'm sure you'll find this exercise amusing—and beneficial—as you become aware of liaisons in your own language.   This simple exercise will help bring the reality of this language phenomenon closer to your own experience; it will, as we say in English, "bring it closer to home."   Seeing it at work in your native Chinese will help you to more readily accept it—and use it—in English!

2) Expressing the whole verb, not just half

It's of prime importance— when encountering verbs—that you focus on **the whole verb**, whether it's "a 2-word verb" or any other English verb you encounter.   As we have discussed, students are likely to look only at the first part of a verb, but ignore the second part—the preposition— that often follows it.   They will, for example, zero in on the verb, "participate," but ignore the preposition that follows, the preposition that completes the verb, that expresses the whole idea, i.e. "participate **in**."   They will see "respond," but ignore the preposition that completes the verb, that expresses the whole verb, i.e., "respond **to**."

As with "2-word verbs," the student is erroneously focusing only on a single word, while ignoring the second important element of the verb—the preposition—that is, in fact, an integral part of the verb, that makes the verb whole!   Please keep in mind that the verb is NOT just "inquire," but "inquire **about.**"   Again, may I suggest that you widen your view so that you always include the preposition that completes the verb, that is, I repeat, a part of the verb?

Therefore, when reading or when you click on your online dictionaries to look up a verb you don't know, widen your view, be sure to pay equal—careful—attention to the preposition that often accompanies the verb in question.   In other words, if you read or look up the word "adjust," be sure to pay close attention to the "second little word" that is, in fact, a part of the verb, thus, "adjust **to**."   (Keep in mind that the verb is not simply "adjust," but "adjust **to**.") If you read or look up the word "rely," be sure to pay close attention to the "second little word" that is, in fact, a part of the verb, thus, "rely **on**."   (Keep in mind that the verb is not just "rely," but "rely **on**").   Again, view and

learn the two words as though they were one word.   In other words:

two words, but one verb!   Ergo, "reply **to**," "think **about**," "aim **at**,"

"arrange **for**," "devoted **to**," etc.   Believe me, this practice will pay

you huge dividends.   As a result, you will not omit the all-important

"second little word" in speaking or writing because you have learned

"reply to" as though it were 1 word.   No more will you say or write, "I

inquired his family." or "I replied his email."   Your English will be

easily understood by native speakers.   You will be expressing your

intelligence.   (We will discuss this same principle as it applies to

nouns in *Part VI: Some thoughts on Vocabulary*).

Keep in mind

As indicated above, prepositions—like articles—will, very

likely, be present in most English sentences and questions.   Make it a

point, then, to put your attention on them and "how" they are used.   If,

for example, you encounter in your reading a sentence such as:

The President returned to Capitol Hill on Friday to deliver

a keynote speech to the members of Congress,

take special note of ("return **to**," "**on** Friday," "**to** the members," etc.)

As prepositions play a major role in English, pay close attention to them in all your investigations, whether reading, listening or speaking.   In doing so, you will naturally get a "feel" for them.   With each passing day, you will become increasingly aware of their importance.   You'll begin to use them with ease.   Please avoid skimming over them as if they didn't exist.   As these LITTLE words play a BIG role in English, they are essential for clear and accurate communication.   Your mastery of English depends on using them correctly.

Part V

Pronunciation! Pronunciation! Pronunciation!
or Your Pronunciation Will Make You or Break You

Pronunciation is integral to all language learning

As we have just seen, pronunciation plays a major role in "2-word verbs."   Allow me to stress that clear pronunciation is critical to your success in mastering English.   Its importance cannot be overstressed!   As stated above, pronunciation will make you or break you.   Allow me to put it this way: what good does it do you, dear student, if you understand English grammar inside out and outside in, if you have a vocabulary that stretches from your hometown in China to Philadelphia, but native speakers of English have difficulty in understanding you because your pronunciation is poor?   And yet, I have found—again, I beg your pardon for my frankness—that this is often the case with Chinese students.   Clear pronunciation is as important to your success as grammar and vocabulary!   Please keep this valuable advice at the fore of your mind.

Cautionary Tale 1: "Vine Street"

Why do I stress pronunciation?   Let me share with you an experience that I recently had.   A Chinese graduate student— courageously and honestly—admitted to me that a cab driver in Philadelphia did not understand him when he attempted to say, "Vine Street."   His pronunciation was so poor that the cab driver could not understand him.   (Often when in such situations, Chinese students will resort to spelling words to their native-English listeners.   This, dear student, is a self-defeating practice; I STRONGLY URGE YOU TO AVOID IT AT ALL COSTS!

Such experiences as this are not rare for Chinese students. They are the result of neglecting pronunciation in favor of stressing grammar rules, memorizing vocabulary and passing standardized exams.

Please keep in mind that pronunciation is integral to all language learning and should be stressed in all your investigations. Always include pronunciation.   Be careful not to allow it to fall by the wayside.   POOR PRONUNCIATION WILL UNDERMINE ALL YOUR EFFORTS TO MASTER ENGLISH.   I can honestly say that all the grammatical work we have done to this point will be as nothing, if you don't have clear pronunciation.

Four vital pronunciation points

Following are four major points of pronunciation that will surely put you in alignment with American English, that will surely put the right map in your hands!   Integrating these four important sounds of American English into your spoken English has two important advantages:

1) native speakers will more readily understand you and, in turn,

2) you will have greater ease in understanding them.

These pronunciation points of American English will open your ears!   They will aid you in being in harmony with what English really is.   Unfortunately, pronunciation in a classroom environment, is often pushed aside, treated as though it were an isolated aspect of language learning.   This is akin to teaching music separate from rhythm and melody!   Rhythm and melody are integral—there's that word, again—to music.   In the same way, pronunciation is integral to all language learning.   Please remember that pronunciation is always present—or should always be present—no matter what aspect of English you are working on.   If you're working on grammar, pronunciation is there, if you're working on vocabulary, pronunciation is there.   Again, I repeat: pronunciation should always be at the fore of your mind.

In music, we aim to hit the right notes.   It's no different in learning a new language.   We aim, through pronunciation, to hit the right sounds.   Please, don't neglect pronunciation.   Please don't treat it as an appendage to learning English.   I repeat, if you are learning a grammar point, pronunciation should be there!   If you are learning vocabulary, pronunciation should be there!   As noted above, pronunciation is a fundamental component of language learning. Therefore, make pronunciation an integral part of all your investigations.   This is an essential principle.   And, please, please don't limit yourself by thinking that you can't pronounce English correctly because you're not a native speaker.   This is self-defeating, erroneous thinking.   Please keep in mind our discussion of ABCs.

For your well-being and success in mastering English, I implore you, dear student, to consider and integrate the following points of pronunciation in all your study.   I can safely say that the average Chinese student has little to no understanding of these pronunciation

points.   Stressing these points in all your investigations will be of
great advantage to you.   Please take heed to this "insider's"
understanding.

Pronunciation Point 1:   THE AMERICAN ENGLISH VOWEL SOUND (ɑ)

This vowel sound is a major difference between the
pronunciation of American English and British English.   (As we have
discussed, the majority of Chinese students, when studying abroad,
study in the U.S.)   So, let's begin then with this extremely important
American English vowel sound (ɑ).   Using this vowel sound will
provide you with a golden key into everyday American English.   The
use of it will put you in alignment with American English and, thus,
with your American counterparts.   In other words, you will be on the
same wavelength as native speakers in the U.S.

Here is the very root of much confusion between Chinese
speaker and American listener!   Chinese students are taught the
British pronunciation of this vowel /ɒ/ which differs
CONSIDERABLY from the American pronunciation /ɑ/.   Please
consider the following examples:

American English says, "h/a/t", not "h/ɒ/t"

American English says, "l/a/t", not "l/ɒ/t"

American English says, "st/a/p" not "st/ɒ/p"

A major difference, wouldn't you agree?   The list goes on and on.   And, yes, American English says "/a/n and /ɑ/n," not "/ɒ/n and /ɒ/n."   American English says,

"l/a/gical," not "l/ɒ/gical,"

"p/a/sitive," not "p/ɒ/sitive,"

"sh/a/pping," not "sh/ɒ/pping"

"p/a/litics," not "p/ɒ/litics"

"pr/a/ject," not "pr/ɒ/ject"

And, believe it or not, dear student, American English says,

"s/a/rry," not "s/ɒ/rry"

The letter "o" in American English tends to sound "/ɑ/."   I wish I could assure you that every letter "o" in American English is pronounced the same, but I can't, because it isn't.   However, I can assure you that you will be heading in the right direction, you will have the right concept, if you approach the letter "o" with the sound of /ɑ/. (I'd venture to say that the vowel sound /ɑ/ for the letter "o" occurs more frequently than any of the other vowel sounds for the letter "o").

Again, in learning and using this pronunciation, you will have an "entry" into American English, you will have the right map in your hands, you will reach your destination with greater ease.   Please trust me in this.

Try this.

I invite you at this time to take a few minutes and first say aloud "cl/ɑ/ck", then say "cl/ɒ/ck."   Again, do you hear what I mean? They are two very different sounds.   I would highly recommend that you repeat this exercise—aloud—with all the examples listed above. No doubt, you'll understand why I stress the importance of learning this frequently-reoccurring American vowel sound.

Being in alignment

I trust that you can now see that your understanding and progress are hindered considerably—particularly in the beginning and intermediate levels—if you are thinking "g/ɒ/t" and your American counterparts are saying "g/ɑ/t," if you're thinking "J/ɒ/hn" and your American counterparts are saying, "J/ɑ/hn," if you're thinking "n/ɒ/t," and your American counterparts are saying, "n/ɑ/t."   Quite simply, you won't readily understand what you hear. Why? Because you won't be in harmony with American English; you won't be aligned with the language of the (American) environment. You'll be thinking one sound and hearing another. How can you make progress if you are thinking and saying the "wrong" sound, if you're thinking and saying /ɒ/, and Americans are saying /ɑ/. So, don't you think it wise to learn this fundamental American vowel sound? In so doing, you'll be aligned with what English really is (in the U.S.!). You'll have the correct view, you'll be traveling in the right direction; your path will be smoother, easier!

This is a major, concrete example where learning British English puts you at a disadvantage. This is an instance where learning British English will have you looking through the wrong end of the telescope (!), consequently, retarding your progress and understanding, not to mention creating confusion for both you and your American listener!

Your small electric appliance

Allow me to explain it this way. Let's say you come to the U.S. with a small electrical appliance such as a hairdryer. As you

know, you won't be able to plug the appliance into an American outlet.
The plug prongs are different; they don't line up.   The current is
different!   They are essentially incompatible.   British English (the
Chinese plug) is incompatible with American English (the American
outlet).   Please understand that this is not chauvinism on my part; it's
practical.   Once again, I think it's fair to say that the majority of
Chinese students and business people will be dealing with Americans
in their college, personal and professional lives.   So, doesn't it make
sense to learn American English so that you will be aligned with your
American friends and colleagues?

George Bernard Shaw (1856-1950), like Oscar Wilde, saw the
truth of this matter when he wittily observed:

England and America are two countries separated by the same

language.

Need I say more?

Pronunciation Point 2:   FINAL CONSONANTS & LIAISONS

ENGLISH LOVES CONSONANT SOUNDS, particularly at
the end of words.   Take a look at an English sentence and you will
soon discover that the majority of words—as in this very sentence—

end in consonant sounds.   Yet, as we have discussed, the Chinese ESL student will have the tendency to "drop" these final consonant sounds. "Talk" becomes "ta" (no [k] sound), "name" becomes "na," (no [m] sound), "light," becomes "li," (no [t] sound), "give" becomes "gi" (no [v] sound), etc.

As we have seen in our discussion of plurals and of "2-word verbs," this "dropping" of the final consonant sound in English— occurs because the Chinese language doesn't have consonant sounds— or strong consonant sounds—at the end of its words.   Consequently, native Chinese speakers, unconsciously, transfer this pattern to English. As mentioned above, "ta" instead of "take," "na" instead of "name," etc.

To complicate the matter, students often "think" they're pronouncing the final consonant sound, when, in fact, they aren't. (They "hear" it in their mind, but fail to actually pronounce it when speaking).   Please do not consider this is a permanent condition! With awareness and practice on your part, it will become—like riding a bike and using chopsticks—second nature to you.   Therefore, in all your investigations, I would highly recommend that you work on this all-important aspect of English pronunciation.

Revisiting liaisons

To ease your way into this pronunciation, let's revisit "liaisons." In Concept 10, we investigated the liaisons that exist between most "2-word verbs." Liaisons also occur WHENEVER ANY ENGLISH WORD THAT ENDS IN A CONSONANT IS FOLLOWED BY A WORD THAT BEGINS WITH A VOWEL.

Following are some examples of this liaison in everyday, American English. And yes, this phenomenon occurs in British English, Canadian English, Australian English, etc. As we have seen, it's a major feature of language, be that language English or Chinese!

English says, "o-nit," not "on   it"

English says, "a lo-dof," not "a   lot   of"

English says, "rea-dit," not "read   it"

English says, "it-za," not "it's   a"

English says, "ha-va," not "have   a"

English says, "doe-zit," not "does   it"

English says, "ta-ka," not "take   a"

English says, "an-da," not "and   a"

I invite you at this point to read the above examples aloud, again, listening carefully to yourself.   This simple exercise will provide you with understanding—and worthwhile practice—in this all-important pronunciation.

What's more, since the above examples are everyday spoken English, used with great frequency by native speakers, you should have no difficulty in hearing them repeatedly and, thus, integrating them into your own conversation.

Once you master the above examples, you will discover that you spontaneously begin to hear other liaisons.   These, you will find, will be far easier to master and integrate into your everyday speech. They will, subsequently, become a part of your natural, growing, correct, clear pronunciation.   BE SURE TO LISTEN FOR THEM AND TO USE THEM WHEN SPEAKING ENGLISH.

I repeat: focusing on this aspect of spoken English will help you to eliminate the "dropping" of consonant sounds at the end of words. As we've seen, it will also eliminate the "staccato"/choppiness from your spoken English.   It will align you to what English really is, facilitating your understanding as well as being clearly understood by native speakers.

Practicing liaisons

Take a look at a short article online or even an ad, and highlight the words where a liaison exists.   Remember, liaisons will always take place where the "first word" ends in a consonant and the "second word" begins with a vowel.

Example 1: If you read a sentence such as:

Joe and I went to the movies,

look for instances where liaisons occur, then underline them.   In the above example, it would be, "an<u>d I</u>."   Pronounce it aloud: "an-dI." Follow this with a sentence of your own and, again, read it aloud:

Phil an<u>d I</u> are old friends.

Example 2: If you read a sentence such as:

My new job is very interesting,

look for instances where liaisons occur, then underline them.   In the above example, it would be, "jo<u>b is</u>."   Pronounce it aloud: "jo-bis." Follow this with a sentence of your own and, again, read it aloud:

Charlie's new jo<u>b is</u> rewarding.

Example 3: If you read a question such as:

Did she give it to them?

look for examples where liaisons occur, then underline them.   In the

above sentence, it would be, "gi<u>ve it</u>."   Pronounce it aloud: "gi<u>ve it</u>."

Follow this with a question of your own and, again, read it aloud:

Did she gi<u>ve it </u>to Chris?

Be alert to liaisons in all your investigations, whether you are

reading or in conversation with native speakers of English.   Listen for

them when watching movies!   They will always be there!   I repeat,

this practice will yield benefits for you in understanding others as well

as in being clearly understood!   I repeat, how can you make progress,

how can you understand correctly, if you are thinking/saying one sound

while native speakers are saying another?

Pronunciation Point 3: "th" (θ) and "th" (ð)

I recently watched a video of eight Chinese students, both

undergraduate and graduate, discussing their experiences and

challenges as international students, living and studying in the U.S.

Without exception, every one of them said, *"I sink _____," "I*

sink _____," "I sink _____."   "Sink," dear student, in

English has two meanings.

As a noun, it means a ceramic basin—in either the kitchen or bathroom—with water faucets to wash dishes or your hands, e.g.

The kitchen sink is full of dirty dishes.

As a verb, it means to go (far) below the surface of water, mud, snow, e.g.,

The car began to sink in the mud.

Obviously, these well-meaning, intelligent students meant, "I think" and, yes, we all understood what they meant, but "I sink" is not correct English pronunciation.

"That's not what I meant!"

Please consider this often heard Chinese English:

Example 1: (actual student pronunciation)

*"He put it in his **mouse**."*

(The student meant to say, "He put it in his mou**th**," but actually said, "He put it in his mou**se**.")   No doubt, you will agree there is a big difference in meaning!

Example 2: (actual student pronunciation)

*"This Great Wall of China has very **sick** walls."*

(The student meant to say, "This Great Wall of China has very **thick** walls." but actually said, "This Great Wall of China has very **sick** walls.") Yet again, I'm sure you would agree that there is a big difference!

Example 3: (actual student pronunciation)

*"Which one is the **turd**?"*

(The student meant to say, "Which one is the **th**ird?" but actually said, "Which one is the **t**urd?")   Oh, dear, how embarrassing!   Big difference, right?

Example 4: (actual student pronunciation)

*"**Sank** you."*

(The student meant to say, *"**Th**ank you,"* but actually said, *"**Sank** you."*)   I trust you now understand what I mean.

θ and ð are here to stay

The point I would like to stress here is this: the "th" sounds (θ) and (ð) occur, as you well know, with great frequency in English. Great frequency!   These sounds are an integral part of the sound system of English.   And, they are here to stay!   They are not going away; they are not going to disappear.   They've been a part of the

English language for centuries and, most likely, will continue to be so.
So, why not concentrate on them in all your investigations?   So, why
not learn to articulate them correctly—once and for all—and grow in
confidence, knowing that you are saying what you actually mean?

    Yes, I know they are not part of the sound system of Chinese,
but this doesn't mean—as we have previously discussed—that you
cannot learn them.   Let's remember that we, as human beings, have
the ability to change!   What's more, we all have the same
"equipment" i.e., the same musculature: tongues, lips, teeth, etc. to
pronounce new and different sounds.   We only have to access the
"new" sound in ourselves.   In other words, we have first to listen
carefully and then attempt to "find" the sound—make the articulation—
in ourselves.   Let me assure you that it is there.   And please let me
remind you that these sounds are only "different," not "difficult."
Aim to free yourself.   Free yourself from the erroneous mindset that
tells you that only native speakers of English can articulate these
sounds.   (Please remember the example of the ABCs; they essentially
have native-speaker pronunciation in both Chinese and English!).
Free yourself so that you can spontaneously say "mouth"—not
"mouse"— when you mean "mouth," to say "faith"—not "face"—

when you mean *"faith,"* to say *"thick"*—not *"sick"*—when you mean *"thick,"* to say *"thank you"*—not *"sank you"*—when you mean *"thank you."* In short, make friends with these quintessentially English sounds. You can do it!

Pronunciation is always present

I do not exaggerate when I say that the pronunciation of *th* (θ) and ($\eth$) should be integrated in all your investigations, always kept at the fore of your mind. As these sounds do not exist in Chinese, you should practice them until—as we've pointed out—they become second nature to you. To neglect the importance of this pronunciation is to invite misunderstanding and confusion, to cheat yourself from reaching your full potential. As we have stated previously, pronunciation is always present—or should be—no matter the topic. When you're studying grammar, pronunciation is there. When you're studying vocabulary, pronunciation is there. Pronunciation is always present! Please do not treat it as though it were a separate— unimportant, secondary— skill. I repeat, pronunciation is integral to all language learning.

As aforementioned, we now live in the world of the Internet where you have immediate access to vast sources of information 24/7. You have the advantage of seeing and hearing English spoken in a wide range of formats: news broadcasts, ads, movies, etc.   You can even go to "youku.com" or "youtube.com" and access instruction on the articulation of (θ) and (ð)!   Thus, there is no reason why any ESL student should—in this day and age—say *"force"* when he actually means *"fourth,"* why any student should say "seem" when she actually means *"theme."*   Awareness and practice it takes, yes!   Awareness, practice and a sincere interest to master English.

Pronunciation Point 4: CONTRACTIONS

In everyday spoken English, Americans ALWAYS use contractions.   It is the natural, spontaneous way of speaking English. Let's take a look at this more closely:

Native speakers say, *"He's going,"* not "He is going."

Native speakers say, *"It's two o'clock,"* not "It is two o'clock."

Native speakers say, *"I'd like to go,"* not "I would like to go."

Native speakers say, *"I'm hungry,"* not "I am hungry."

Native speakers say, *"I can't,"* not "I cannot."

Native speakers say, "*She'll do it*," not "She will do it."

Yet, most Chinese students—and please allow me to repeat that I am not criticizing, only pointing out their misconceptions—almost never use contractions in speaking English.   Yet again, failure to use contractions hinders your understanding to everyday spoken English. Failure to understand and use contractions keeps you out of out of alignment with your English-speaking counterparts.   Allow me to elaborate.

Two different sounds

As in the case of the pronunciation of the vowel sounds (/ɑ/ and /ɒ/), you won't readily understand "don't," if you're—erroneously— thinking "do not."   The two sounds are completely different.   They are, in fact, two different utterances.   Please take a moment now and say aloud,

"do not,"

Good!   Now say,

"don't."

See what I mean?   Hear what I mean?   THEY ARE TWO DIFFERENT SOUNDS!   They are, in fact, two distinct utterances.

If you're thinking

"could not,"

you will not readily understand

"couldn't."

Why?   Because THEY ARE TWO DIFFERENT SOUNDS!   They

are, in fact, two distinct utterances.

If you're thinking

"did not,"

and the native speaker of English says,

"didn't,"

you will not readily grasp "didn't," because THEY ARE TWO

DIFFERENT SOUNDS!   They're two distinct utterances.

So, put yourself on the same wavelength as everyday spoken

English by using contractions in your everyday conversations.

Contractions are standard spoken English in the USA, the UK and, yes,

in Canada, Australia and New Zealand, too!   Like liaisons,

contractions are a major feature of spoken English!

Additionally, failure to use contractions in everyday speech causes—again—an increased "staccato"/choppiness in your spoken English.   Using contractions—when speaking—will not only facilitate your understanding of spoken English, it will also put you in in alignment with your native speaker counterparts.   You will be on the same page as native speakers!   Using contractions will give you another "entry" into what English really is.   You will have the right perspective!

PLEASE TAKE NOTE: Though contractions are used in everyday spoken English, they are, as a rule, avoided in formal writing. (By formal writing, I mean college essays, business correspondence, professional articles, etc.,).

Pronunciation passport

To sum up, these four vital pronunciation points will open your ears to clearly hear what is being said in the American English environment.   As we have previously stated, they will provide you with an "entry" into spoken English.   We might even say that these four points are a "pronunciation passport" to everyday spoken English in the US.   Being aware of these sounds, it will then follow that you will hear them and pronounce them correctly.   You will be in tune!   I repeat, you will be in harmony with English.

A word to the wise! 4

Again, successful language learning requires a willingness to expand one's way of thinking; a willingness to walk in another's shoes, a fearlessness; a willingness to put aside what we are used to and to try something new.   Pronunciation provides us the opportunity to practice these qualities.   This positive, open attitude is as important to you as grammar and vocabulary.   It's the great enabler!

Oh, one last thing about pronunciation

Following are two everyday English words that Chinese students often mispronounce.   I include them here so that you will learn them and thus be well prepared when you reach our shores:

- "because," in standard American English, is pronounced [biˈkəz], not [biˈkoz]

- "usually," in standard American English, is pronounced [juʒəwəli], not [ˈju ju li]

Insights into Successful Learning 7

Language is economical

As we have stressed, students often have misconceptions about English.   They tend to have a stiff, inflexible view of the language. This, more often than not, is the result—as we have discussed—on an overemphasis on grammar rules and isolated vocabulary.   Let's take a look at some examples of stiff, unnatural English to show you just what I mean.   In doing so, I hope to help you become aware of the debilitating effects of—only—textbook learning.   Here we go.

If you ask the average Chinese student,

"How many books do you have in your backpack?",

she, most likely, will answer,

"I have 4 books in my backpack."

A native speaker of English would simply answer,

"4"

Ask a Chinese student,

"Where are you going?"

and he will, probably, give a grammar book response,

"I am going home."

A native speaker, however, would simply answer,

"home."

(This is akin to our comments in **Concept 5, "Answering questions: a round peg in a round hole"**).

The Chinese student's answers reflect textbook English, an English that tends to be divorced from everyday, spontaneous, living English. (Remember our discussion: **English is Alive!**) As has been pointed out, grammar book English tends to keep you "in a suit of armor," to distance you from what English really is. It does not put you in harmony with the language; it often gives you mistaken ideas about English.

Unintentionally misguided

Before we continue with our discussion of this topic, allow me to repeat that I am not belittling Chinese students nor splitting hairs. Allow me to stress that the Chinese student answers the question incorrectly because his grammar book—most likely—has given him a mistaken perspective. He has been a good student, he has been obedient, he has learned what he has been told. The problem, however, is that he has not been given the correct information, the correct understanding.   (As we indicated at the outset, this is akin to putting the wrong information in your GPS!)

Again, my purpose is to share with you what English really is, so that you can avoid the perils that you will face when you absorb lifeless grammar rules.   In other words, to point out to you where you are not in alignment with English so that you can, in turn, change your perspective and, thereby, become attuned to English.

Sadly, stressing rigid grammar rules and isolated vocabulary items creates a disconnect between you and the living language; it tends to foster a distorted view of English.   Consequently, misconceptions—and mistakes—abound.   Allow me to remind you that if you rely solely on a grammar book perspective, you will find yourself "in a suit of armor," in hard and fast rules which will shut you out from the living language that is being spoken in the "here and now."

Awakening to the economy of language: a simple reflection

Take a moment—right now—and ask yourself in your native Chinese (please don't think about it, but simply say what spontaneously comes to your mind) the following question. Are you ready? Okay, here we go.

Question 1: "Where are you from?"

Be honest with yourself! What was your spontaneous answer in Chinese? Was it,

"I am from China"

or was it,

"China?"

I bet it was simply *"China"*.

Now, try this.

Question 2: Ask yourself in Chinese,

"What's your major?"

Again, I ask you to be honest with yourself, to say what first comes to mind. What was your spontaneous answer? Was it,

"My major is architecture."

or simply

"architecture?"

I bet it was *"architecture."*

Dr. Gattegno pointed out that this short answer is a basic human behavior, explaining that all language is—in his word—"economical."

People are not foolish.   None of us will use more energy in speaking—or in anything else for that matter—than is necessary! Ponder this and you'll discover that it's true.   Ponder it a little deeper and it will open your mind to a new view of learning, a new view of English.

An important insight: "chi"

"Chi," as you know, is a Chinese word, a Chinese concept.   It reflects an acute Chinese awareness of life.   But what, you may ask yourself, does it has to do with learning English?   A lot!

To clarify my point, let's take a look at the experience of dissecting a frog in biology class.   Sound strange?   Well, it really isn't.   Like the piano lesson, it's relevant to learning English.

In biology class, the student dissects a frog and studiously learns all the names of the organs, their functions, etc.   Yet, in spite of all his effort, in spite of all the "knowledge" that he has attained, he has, in reality, overlooked a major factor.   He has neglected to consider the invisible life force which is the very essence of all life! The biology student thinks he's studying life, but he's actually studying the absence of life because he's focusing on a dead frog!   He has, in the course of his study, neglected to recognize the invisible—yet ever-present—force that animates all of life.   He has overlooked what Chinese acupuncturists and healers have for millennia seen and honored at the very heart of life: chi.

How this applies to learning English

When grammatical rules and the memorization of vocabulary are overstressed, we are, in essence, studying a dead frog!   We have neglected to see and use—the vital life force, the chi—that is inherent in all of life, whether we are talking about health, biology, calligraphy, tai chi (!), painting, music or language learning.

Is it any wonder then that students—overburdened by rote learning i.e., "studying a dead frog"—have difficulty in speaking English and, when they do, it's mechanical, robot-like?

I have often observed students approach a sentence as if it were a mathematical formula, i.e., "This kind of word goes here and that kind of word goes there," without having any understanding of the word and its relationship to other words in a sentence, without having a "feel" for English.   Please remember that English, like every language, is alive!   Therefore, please do not approach your study of English as if it were a dead frog!

Lao Tzu's profound insight rings true again:

Enumerate the parts of a carriage

and you have not defined the carriage.

I, therefore, implore you to carefully consider this all-important point of "chi."   I feel sure it will add life to your learning.   I'm sure it will add life to your English!   Please keep the "chi" of English—the "chi" of learning—at the very heart of your investigations.   Let's keep in mind that language is in life, not in a textbook.   Let's keep in mind that English is in life, not in a textbook.   I repeat: it is my sincere hope that by pointing out the major misconceptions that Chinese students tend to have that you will, in turn, arrive at the right concept of English, that you will be in touch with the spirit of English, that you will have a clearer understanding of what English really is, that you will make noteworthy progress.

Part VI

Some Thoughts on Vocabulary

Reminder: vocabulary is only part of the picture

Throughout this book, we have discussed the importance of mastering the grammatical structures of English.   We've seen that the grammatical structures of any language take precedence over vocabulary.   I emphasize this because my experience, as I have previously indicated, has shown that many students are often under the false assumption that learning English is simply a matter of memorizing lists of vocabulary words.   Please keep in mind that NOTHING, DEAR STUDENT, COULD BE FURTHER FROM THE TRUTH.

As we have pointed out, memorizing the dictionary from cover to cover, will not serve you in mastering English.   Allow me to remind you that by doing so, you will end up attaching English words to Chinese grammatical structures.   Memorizing vocabulary without considering the crucial role of grammatical structures will keep you locked into speaking and writing Chinese English.   It will keep you thinking only in Chinese.   Result: your spoken and written English will often be difficult to understand, often incomprehensible.   (Please remember that English is not a word-for-word translation of Chinese just as Chinese is not a word-for-word translation of English).

Sadly, an overemphasis on vocabulary often results in the Chinese student uttering isolated words with little to no English sentence structure or meaning!   (Please keep in mind "You need a cup to hold your tea").   Let's investigate!

A student who has made it a priority to memorize lists of isolated words will tend to make single-word utterances such as,

"Yeah, yeah, evaluation"

which, in essence, means very little. "What", English asks, "are you talking about?"   "Are you going to make an evaluation?"   "Did you make an evaluation?"   "Do you have to make an evaluation?"   "Are you planning on making an evaluation?" etc.   Additionally, memorizing lists of isolated vocabulary will result in sentences like, "Even he doesn't know the rules," or questions like, "How to pronounce?"

Please keep in mind that language is not only a matter of WHAT is expressed, but HOW it's expressed.   "What" and "how" ALWAYS go together.   As we have seen, they are true partners!   Be sure not to "divorce" them.   Again, I ask that you please trust me in this.   Please remember that "how" is as important as "what."   As previously stressed, be sure to make this vital relationship between "how" and "what" an integral part of all your investigations.

Alert: 2 different things!

Therefore, when approaching vocabulary, it's of the utmost importance to realize that IT'S ONE THING TO KNOW "WHAT" A WORD MEANS, QUITE ANOTHER TO KNOW "HOW" TO USE IT CORRECTLY IN A SENTENCE OR QUESTION.   This essential principle cannot be overemphasized.   It's self-defeating to memorize lists of words without knowing how to use them correctly.   This counterproductive practice is akin to learning numbers, but not knowing how to use them.   In other words, it's akin to memorizing numbers, but not knowing how to add, subtract, multiply, divide.   For the sake of your progress, then, I wholeheartedly recommend that you avoid burying yourself in lists of vocabulary words without knowing how to use them correctly.   In learning any new vocabulary item, be sure that you know how to use it correctly in a sentence or question. Once you learn a new word, make it a regular practice to write a sentence or question, maybe even 2 or 3, with the new vocabulary item.

If you have any doubts as to its accuracy, consult your teacher, whom

I'm sure will be delighted that you've asked him!

Using the dictionary

When using a dictionary, it's of vital importance that you

consult an authoritative source, whether it's a Chinese English or just

English dictionary.   An authoritative dictionary will not only give you

the correct meaning(s) of a word, it will often provide you with a few

example sentences that will show you how the word is used.

PLEASE REMEMBER THAT IT'S ONE THING TO KNOW

"WHAT" A WORD MEANS, QUITE ANOTHER TO KNOW

"HOW" TO USE IT CORRECTLY IN A SENTENCE OR

QUESTION.   Take the time to study the examples that the dictionary

offers.   They will open doors for you!

Dictionary and thesaurus

And while we've discussing dictionaries, let me warn you that

many online Chinese English sources/dictionaries are NOTORIOUSLY

INACCURATE!   THEREFORE, BE SURE TO CHOOSE A

RELIABLE SOURCE.   This is equally true for online translations. The definitions and translations are often so ludicrous as to cause a native speaker of English to double over with laughter!   (No doubt, the same thing occurs when translating from English to Chinese!) Yet, Chinese students often use these unauthoritative online sources as though they were the gospel truth!   So, be wise, be extremely careful when using online dictionaries and translations!

I highly recommend hard copies, i.e., books.   Books will always provide you with more thorough explanations and, of equal importance, you won't be distracted by annoying advertising that hinders your concentration.   *The Oxford Advanced Learner's Dictionary* as well as *The American Heritage Dictionary of the English Language* are excellent, reliable, authoritative sources.   (You might also check out any of Oxford's English Chinese Dictionary publications).   Having reputable resources at your fingertips is essential for your success as English learners.   I know it's easier to click your mouse than to open a book and look up the word you don't understand, but, if you take the time to open the book, your efforts will—in the long run—be of greater benefit to your understanding and progress.   Again, please trust me in this.

And, please familiarize yourself with a thesaurus.   A thesaurus, like a good dictionary, is an invaluable help to you, particularly in improving your writing skills.

Cautionary tale 2: Unreliable online sources

Recently, I worked with a Chinese student on her cover letter. She wanted to express that she had worked with an "Advertising Art Director" in China.   She did not know how to say "Advertising Art Director" in English, so she submitted her inquiry to an online translation website.   It gave her "Propaganda Minister!"   Dear student, need I say more?   Therefore, please use a reliable dictionary or an authoritative online source.   (Again, printed dictionaries are in my experience superior to online sources and will greatly aid you in mastering English).

Keep an eye out: nouns that can also be verbs.

In all your dictionary investigations, BE ON THE LOOKOUT FOR NOUNS THAT CAN ALSO BE VERBS.   For instance, if you look up the noun "harvest," you will be pleasantly surprised to discover that "harvest" can also be used as a verb.

Keeping this feature of English in mind, you will soon come to realize that many of the nouns you already know can be used as verbs. You will be delighted to discover, for example, that the noun "milk" can also be a verb as in

Dairy farmers milk their cows twice a day,

that the noun "butter," likewise, can be a verb as in

Americans usually butter their toast.

Or that the search engine, "Google" can be a verb as in

If you don't know an answer, you can always google it!

This awareness will cause a major shift in your thinking; it will, by its very nature, open your mind.   You will soon discover that your vocabulary has automatically expanded considerably!   You will soon find yourself questioning every noun you encounter, e.g., "I wonder if 'button' can be a verb."   You may be pleasantly surprised that it can be!   Therefore, keep an eye out for nouns that can also be used as verbs.   A good dictionary, like those recommended above, will make this very clear to you!   (Of course, the opposite is also true: when looking up a verb, check to see if it can be used as a noun!)

Expressing the whole noun

Allow me, once again, to remind you to widen your view, to lengthen the line of your magic marker. As we pointed out in Concept 10, ("Expressing the whole verb, not just half"), the "preposition/the second little word" is an integral part of the verb. This same principle applies to nouns as well. Therefore, in your dictionary investigations, be sure to pay close attention to the word immediately before or after the noun. Let's investigate!

If, for example, you come across the noun, *"exhibition,"* be sure to widen your view to include the word immediately before and after the noun in the example(s) the dictionary or the source material gives. If a sentence reads:

The Philadelphia Museum of Art is mounting an exhibition of

the works of El Greco,

be sure to zero in on *"***an** exhibition **of***"* because the noun, dear student, is actually *"an exhibition of,"* not just *"exhibition."* Likewise, keep an eye on *"***the** works **of**.*"* (Notice, too, that English says "**The** Philadelphia Museum **of** Art").

If, for instance, you look up the noun, *"link,"* extend you magic marker line to include the word immediately before and after the noun in the example(s) the dictionary or the online source material gives.   If

a sentence reads

This website provides a link to the info you need,

be sure to focus on *"***a** link **to***"* because the noun is actually *"a link to,"*

not just "link."   Likewise keep an eye on *"***the** info."   This practice

will, again, pay you big dividends as you will be learning the complete

noun, just as we saw in the case of the complete verb.   No longer will

you say or write:

This website provides link info you need.

(And, if you are alert in your dictionary investigations, you will

discover that the noun *"a link!"* is also a verb).   Ah, the spirit of

English and the joy of learning!

As we have suggested previously, you might follow this up by

writing a short sentence or question with the noun.   If you have any

doubts as to the accuracy of your sentence, again, I recommend that

you ask your teacher.

Quality over quantity

You may feel that these practices take too long, but I can assure

you that they will serve you—very well—in the long run.   Speed and quantity, dear student, are not the point. It's a matter of quality over quantity. What good does it do you to quickly look up a word, understand its meaning, be gratified for the moment, only to forget it the next time you come across it? What good does it do you to understand *"what"* a word means, if you do not know *"how"* to use it correctly? Be patient with yourself. Take your time and you'll be amazed at the progress you'll make.

The Roman historian Valleius Paterculus (c.19 BC – AD 31) wisely tells us:

> *What is quickly accomplished, quickly perishes.*

Again, pronunciation is integral.

And let us not overlook the important fact that pronouncing a word correctly goes hand-in-hand with understanding it and using it correctly. As we have observed, pronunciation is integral to every aspect of language learning. It does you little good if you have an extensive vocabulary, but no one can understand you! As noted before, it's a sad situation when students revert to spelling English words instead of speaking them. Therefore, always keep pronunciation in mind in all your investigations. If you have difficulty pronouncing a given word, do this: write it down, syllable by syllable.

For example, if you have difficulty pronouncing a word like "vocabulary," first, write it down in syllables, as follows: "vo-cab-u-lary." Then, pronounce it—syllable by syllable—until the word flows effortlessly from you. After several such attempts—you decide how many—pronounce it all together, "vocabulary!" Now, wasn't that easy? Be sure to always be patient with yourself.

Many online dictionaries give pronunciation for both American and British English. (Of course, you now know which pronunciation best serves your purpose). Be sure to take advantage of these wonderful resources.

What a difference: British vs American English

One more very important aspect of vocabulary. As you know, I stress the importance of learning American English in today's world. I have pointed out that American English differs considerably from British English in usage, pronunciation and vocabulary. Allow me, at this juncture, to give you a sampling of the differences between everyday American and British English vocabulary.

British English	American English
anticlockwise	counterclockwise
aubergine	eggplant
biscuit	cookie
bonnet (of a car)	hood (of a car)
boot (of a car)	trunk (of a car)
car park	parking lot
chemist	drugstore
cinema	movies
clothes pegs	clothes pins
city centre	downtown
cooker	stove
cotton wool	cotton balls
courgette	zucchini
crisps	potato chips
dressing gown	bathrobe
dual carriageway	divided highway
Father Christmas	Santa Claus
face flannel	washcloth
film	movie
flat	apartment

football	soccer
fortnight	2 weeks
full stop	period
gammon	ham
garden	yard
high street	main street
holiday	vacation
interval	intermission
journey	trip
jumper	sweater
lift	elevator
lorry	truck
main course	entree
muffler	scarf
mum	mom
nappy	diaper
pants	underwear
pavement	sidewalk
petrol	gas
porridge	oatmeal
public school	private school
puncture	flat tire

queue	line
removers	movers
roundabout	traffic circle
row	argument
rucksack	backpack
rubber	eraser
return (ticket)	round trip (ticket)
shop	store
starter	appetizer
surname	last name
sweet	candy
sweet (after main course)	dessert (after entree)
tap	faucet
tin	can
timber	lumber
torch	flashlight
trousers	pants
tube	subway
university	college
way out	exit
waistcoat	exit
zed (the letter "z")	zee (the letter "z")

And this, dear student, is only the tip of the iceberg!   We haven't yet addressed verbs!   Here is a sampling:

British English	American English
to be made redundant	to be laid off
to fetch	to get
to get on with sb	to get along with sb
to give way (traffic sign)	to yield (traffic sign)
to hire (a car)	to rent (a car)
to hoover	to vacuum
to lay the table	to set the table
to let (a flat/house)	to rent (an apartment/house)
to look after	to take care of
to mend	to fix
to post	to mail
to ring	to call
to take away (food from restaurant)	to take out (food from restaurant)
to wash up	to do the dishes

Please bear in mind that the average American would not readily understand the above-mentioned British vocabulary.   (I venture to say that the same holds true for the average English person; he would not readily understand the American English!)   Let's recall the insights of Oscar Wilde and George Bernard Shaw (see page 15 and 191).   Is it any wonder that they made such remarks?   Their perception is not only witty, it's absolutely true!   Need I say any more then about the importance of learning American English in today's world?   Please keep in mind that the majority of Chinese students, when studying abroad, study in the US.

Essential classroom vocabulary: 1) Punctuation Marks and 2) Parts of Speech

1) Punctuation Marks

Although Chinese students are familiar with the basic punctuation marks, they—unfortunately—do not know the English names for these symbols.   (If they know anything, they know "full stop" which, as we have just seen, is British English, and has next to no meaning for the average American).

If I say to a Chinese student, "This sentence needs quotation marks," he will look at me with a blank expression.   I then proceed to explain, only to hear, "Oh, I know that word in Chinese."   Well, that's wonderful, but, chances are, your English professor in the host country doesn't speak Chinese!

Likewise, students tend not to know the English word *"punctuation."* If, for instance, I say to a Chinese student—and I mean an advanced student of English—"This sentence needs punctuation," he will look at me, once again, with a blank expression!

Let's attempt, then, to address this important—useful— vocabulary to eliminate this debilitating oversight.

Vocabulary for punctuation marks: your computer keyboard is your guide!

As regards the vocabulary for punctuation, let your computer keyboard be your guide. It's all there!

a period [.], a comma [,], a question mark [?], an exclamation mark [!], a colon [:], a semicolon [;], quotation marks ["], an apostrophe ['], a hyphen [-], a forward slash [/], a hashtag [#], parenthesis [(,)].

(Please notice that English says, *"a period," "a question mark," "a colon," etc., not "period," "question mark," "semicolon,"* etc.) Thus, learning the names of the punctuation marks will provide additional opportunities for you to practice "a."   It will provide an

opportunity to reinforce the importance of "a" in English.

2) Parts of Speech

Knowing the English expression, "part of speech" as well as the

names for the individual parts of speech is akin to knowing the English

names for punctuation marks!   The vocabulary for the parts of speech

is, at times, essential for communication between teacher and student,

particularly again, in an overseas English class.   I am the last teacher

on the face of the earth to burden students with grammatical

terminology, but I feel that a basic vocabulary for the parts of speech

facilitates understanding and addressing (many) grammatical issues.

Vocabulary for the parts of speech

Following is a short list of the parts of speech that you should

know in English:

a noun, a verb, an adjective, an adverb, a pronoun,

a preposition, an article

(Again, please notice that English says *"a noun," "a verb,"*

"an adjective," "an adverb," etc., not *"noun," "verb," "adjective,"*

etc.).   Thus, learning the names of the parts of speech will, like
learning the names of punctuation marks, provide additional
opportunities for you to practice "a."   It will provide you an
opportunity to reinforce the importance of "a" in English.   Again,
integrated learning!

The infinitive

Last, but certainly not least, the part of speech called "*the
infinitive.*"   Please do not be put off by this "unfriendly user name."
It simply refers to the "*to-form*" of any English verb, e.g., *to learn, to
work, to play, to listen,* etc.   That is to say, the infinite is the most
basic form of any English verb, the basic verb form from which all
tenses originate.   For example, *I worked,* originates in the infinite, "to
work;" *she would like,* originates in the infinite, "to like;" *we're
learning,* originates in the infinite, "to learn," etc.   Put another way,
we might say that the infinitive is the trunk of the tree and all verb
tenses are its branches, i.e., all tenses branch from the infinitive.

I don't believe I would be wrong in stating that most students
mistakenly think that the basic form of any English verb is simply,
"sing," "download," "put on," etc.   This, dear student, is another

gross misconception about English. The basic form—the infinitive—of any English verb is, *"***to** sing," not "sing," "**to** download," not "download," "**to** put on" not "put on."

The infinitive, it seems to me, is of vital importance to the native speaker of Chinese who is new to the English concept of tenses. Additionally, a grasp of this basic verb form will help you to understand why English says, *"I want to know,"* not, *"I want know,"* why English says, "He'd like to go," not, "He'd like go."

That's it regarding parts of speech! Nothing complicated, just a simple, correct understanding of the vocabulary that is necessary for your success.

Classroom harmony

Knowing the vocabulary for the punctuation marks and the parts of speech will greatly enhance your learning. Therefore, make it a point to learn this all-important vocabulary so that you can express yourself clearly and intelligently when in English class, so that you can understand what your American professors are referring to. Learning this vocabulary will also enrich your understanding and appreciation of languages and how they work.   Without a doubt, it will facilitate your progress!

Once again, I ask your understanding; I'm not berating Chinese students.   My purpose is to give you a clear picture of what often occurs on this side of the Pacific by explaining another frustrating predicament in which you and your American professors often find yourselves.   It is my hope that by doing so, we can remedy the situation for the well-being of all concerned.

Part VII

A Word about Writing

That sentence is too l-o-n-g: 3 examples of long student sentences, investigated and restructured

Allow me to address another major misconception that Chinese students have. They are generally under the false impression that a good English sentence is a l—o—n—g English sentence. This was true back in the 19th century, but is, generally, no longer the case. It all changed in the twentieth century!

A good English sentence today is concise and to the point. A good English sentence nowadays is simple and clear. You should aim to write succinct sentences of, say, one and a half typewritten lines long. This, I feel, is a good rule of thumb. (If a sentence is longer than one and a half typewritten lines, chances are, it's too long; chances are, it has problems and needs to be separated and adjusted accordingly. If a sentence is two lines long—or over—and contains the word *"and,"* it's *definitely* too long! To show you what I mean, let's investigate a few examples of actual student sentences that are too long.

Actual student sentence 1

"Both projects were complicated since there were too many different

types of campaigns and problems and I was confused how to address

the most suitable topic for my project."

See what I mean?   This sentence has 29 words (!) and contains

the word *"and."*   Both traits are definite indicators that the sentence is

too long and needs attention.   The student's ideas would have been

better expressed by shortening—dividing—the sentence as follows:

Both projects were complicated since there were many different types

of campaigns and problems.   I was confused how to address the most

suitable topic.

By separating the sentence, we create two clearly expressed

ideas.   Each sentence now has its own distinct point; its own sharper

focus.   Notice, too, how we have eliminated wordiness.   First, it's

not necessary to say *"too many"* as *"many"* suffices.   Secondly, *"for*

my project" is likewise unnecessary as we already know that it's for the

student's project.

Actual student sentence 2

Here's another student sentence:

"This category shows data about drunk driving from 1980 till today

and it records how many people were died because of drunk driving

and the punishments of those drunk drivers."

A sentence of 30 words!   And please notice that *"and"* was

used two times! 30 words plus the use of *"and"* two times are both

flashing red lights that readily indicate that the sentence is far too long.

(If you read this sentence aloud, you will soon discover that you will

run out of breath!) The ideas in this too-long sentence could have been

more clearly expressed as follows:

*This category shows **the** data about drunk driving from 1980 till today.*

*It also records how many people were **killed** as well as the **penalties***

the drivers received.

Like the first example, please notice that the sentence has been

divided into two shorter sentences, making the student's ideas clearer.

Please note how the use of *"also"* in the second sentence not only

eliminates *"and,"* but harmoniously ties the second sentence to the

first.   Note, too, that *"as well as"* beautifully replaces the second

"and."   Notice that "penalties" is a better word choice than

"punishment."   (This poor word choice may have been the result of using a unreliable Chinese English online dictionary!) Lastly, the use of the word *"received"* eliminates wordiness.

Actual Student sentence 3

Another example of a far-too-long, student sentence (fasten your seat belts!):

"The motto, "No More Victims" is written in red bold font, which indicates the primary goal of this campaign is to save people's life from drunk drinking and red color can also catch public's attention and give warning from the dangers of drunk driving."

Phew!   A sentence of 44 words!   This is a gross misunderstanding of written English, the student erroneously thinking that a long English sentence is a good English sentence.   Nothing could be farther from the truth!   (Please notice that *"and"* has been used two times!   As previously noted, this is a sure indication that something is amiss!)   It's also the result—in my opinion—of students being in "a suit of armor," confined by rote learning that doesn't allow them to move freely.   This—very—wordy, awkward sentence could be written as follows:

*The motto "No More Victims" is written in a bold red font. This indicates **that** the primary goal of this campaign is **to save lives**. The red **font also** catches the public's attention; it warns of the dangers of drunk driving.*

Now, we have three concise sentences. Notice, dear student, that not only has the sentence been separated into shorter, clearer sentences, but superfluous words have been eliminated. Is it really necessary to say *"people's lives from drunk driving,"* since 1) we already know that the topic of the essay is to save lives from drunk driving and, 2) drunk driving is mentioned in the following sentence. Notice, too, that English doesn't say *"red color,"* it simply says, *"red."* To the English way of thinking, *"red"* is a color, so there's no need to say *"red color."* (*"Red color"* reveals that the student is thinking in Chinese, translating word-for-word from Chinese to English).

The essential point in this discussion is to guide you toward writing shorter, more concise sentences. This is crucial. (Please keep in mind that long sentences tend to be pre-twentieth century English!). Additionally, if you write shorter, more concise sentences, it will be easier for you to express your ideas clearly and to pinpoint your grammatical mistakes.   Please keep in mind, writing concise

sentences will harmonize you to what English really is.

Part VIII

Afterword

Our learning is ongoing

I had first thought of titling this section "In Conclusion," but it occurred to me that in our investigations—as in all things in life—there is no conclusion. If we keep this awareness at the fore of our minds, we will recognize that there is always something new to discover, to learn, something new to work on. If we remain open and aware, our day-to-day investigations will always guide us to the next step. This next step might be a new awareness of English, based on something we heard, read or even said. Of equal importance, it may be a self-awareness, a recognition that we are, for example, over-anxious to learn—"to get it"—that we are exerting too much energy. This, in turn, may impede our progress in spite of our good intentions. In other words, we may actually be getting in the way of our own learning! Here, again, Lao Tzu's wisdom will help us attain the right view:

Practice action without striving.

Freedom and learning

Freedom, to me, is at the heart of life and learning.   It's at the very heart of this book; it's the very theme of this work.   Every idea presented within these pages is an attempt to help free you from the numbing effects of rote learning which is often devoid of intuition, of feeling, of life, while—all too often—ignoring your natural, human awareness, i.e., your natural learning abilities.   In my opinion, if learning—education—does not aim to free us, it's of little use; it's of little value.

Seated at the piano!

Working with the ideas that I have put forth in this book—if carefully considered and practiced—will help to free you from the rigidity of having—only—a grammar book perspective on learning English.   These ideas—these concepts—will help to put you IN the language.   They will help to put you in the atmosphere of living, breathing English.   They will open new vistas.   A sole emphasis on textbooks, sadly, tends to keep you OUT of the language.   As we have seen, it will put you "in a suit of armor."   By following the ideas presented in this book, you will be seated at the piano, your fingers on the keyboard, joyfully learning how to play the music.

It's only ONE tool!

Please keep in mind that a textbook is a tool, but it's only one tool.   So is a hammer!   Fortunately, a carpenter doesn't use only a hammer when he builds.   Imagine how disadvantaged he would be if he had only one tool!   How could he make anything with only a hammer?   Fortunately, he has many different tools and uses them accordingly.   So, then, should you.

Please understand that I'm not suggesting that you throw out the textbook.   I am, however, suggesting that you do not limit yourself to it, that you take your primary gaze off the book, off the page into the fresh air of living, breathing, flexible English.   Let us not forget that stressing the printed page is akin to being able to read the sheet music, but not being able to play the piano!

Spoken vs written language

Though books can help and guide, they are not the source of living language.   The source of living English is in life, itself, in everyday living.   If you want to master English, then make spoken

English your primary focus.   While in China, via the suggestions

we've made in the preceding pages; when in the host country, via

participation in everyday life.

Kindly consider this: Which came first, spoken language or

written language?   As a native speaker of Chinese, did you learn to

speak or read Chinese first?   Obviously, you learned to speak first.

All languages were spoken for millennium before they were written

down.   With this in mind, doesn't it make more sense to focus your

learning on the natural, human side of the spoken language?   Let us

not forget that emphasizing the printed page fosters passive learning,

while emphasizing the spoken language fosters active learning,

understanding and progress.

Cautionary tale 3: "Masters"

Please forgive me for what may seem an impolite remark.   I'm

simply attempting to give you an accurate picture of what often occurs,

as I previously mentioned, on this side of the Pacific, of the

predicament in which Chinese students may unwittingly find

themselves.   Chinese students are likely to be "masters" at passing standardized English tests and, yet, do not speak, write or understand English well.   In other words, high test scores do not ensure fluency, do not ensure success in English.

Consequently, Chinese students are often "lost" on American campuses, unable to express themselves well—either orally or in writing—unable to understand the course content.   (Please remember our friend in Philadelphia and the taxi driver).   Doesn't it make more sense, then, to focus on becoming spontaneous speakers of English? Being a spontaneous user of English is more likely to ensure your success on American campuses as well as in American life, not to mention in being successful test-takers.   May I suggest that you repeatedly question yourself: *Am I learning English to pass standardized tests or to become a competent speaker and writer of English?*   Surely, the answer to this question will put you in the right frame of mind, will give you the right perspective.   Be sure, then, not to put all your time and effort into studying a dead frog!

Edward Carpenter's (1844-1929) keen insight is well worth your consideration:

> *Great success in examinations does not as a rule*
> *naturally go with originality of thought.*

Don't deceive yourself!

In considering the "Concepts" and "Insights for Successful Learning" that I have put forth for you in this book, be careful—very careful—not to deceive yourself into thinking that you—already—know and understand them.   Yes, dear student, you may have been exposed to them, you may recognize them, but do you know how to use them correctly, spontaneously?   You may, for instance, be tempted to think, "Oh yes, I understand plurals," but do you really, do you truly know how to use them correctly, naturally in the "here and now?" Likewise, you may think, "I've seen 'a/an,' 'the' dozens of times, no problem," but do you integrate them in your speaking and writing? My apologies, dear student, but my experience tells me you don't.

To avoid the pitfall of deceiving yourself, be sure that you make a concerted effort into focusing on these "Concepts," and putting them into practice, immediately.   Keep them at the fore of mind.   Avoid procrastinating.   Get on the bike, now!   Sit down at the piano, now! PUT THESE "CONCEPTS" INTO USE **NOW!**   AVOID PASSIVE LEARNING!   BE AN ACTIVE LEARNER!

Once is not enough!

Also, dear student, don't deceive yourself into thinking that you need to read this book only once. That would be a false premise, another major misconception. Be sure to read it again and again. Use it repeatedly as a reference.

If you find, for example, that you continue to omit "a" in your speaking and writing, then reread the section on "a" until it becomes clearer to you, until it becomes second nature to you. Be sure to follow the practical, everyday advice I provide you. You will need to do this if you sincerely want to improve your English. As I pointed out in the beginning, advanced students and working professionals tend to make the very same mistakes, have exactly the same challenges as the intermediate students. Keep in mind that ONCE IS NOT ENOUGH! Go over these concepts repeatedly until they become, as Dr. Gattegno would say, "in your flesh." An intellectual understanding is not enough!

Learning from each other

As stated above, these concepts require a willingness to practice them, to integrate them into your speaking, listening, reading and writing until you can use them spontaneously.

To aid you on your path, may I suggest that you form a group of friends or classmates who meet regularly to discuss issues that you each have.   Do this even if there are only two of you in the group!   Open any English topic to discussion.   The conversation that unfolds—your group investigations—will provide ample opportunity for you and your friends to iron out your doubts, your confusion.

Investigating in this way will help you to better identify your weaknesses.   Once you identify them, you will be in a better place to work on them.   This, in turn, will lead you to a mastery of English.

Please do not underestimate your own abilities.   Work with your friends on the issue at hand until it becomes clear.   You can do it!   Give yourself the chance!   Allow me to stress that by doing so, you will be developing your innate intelligence and intuition, and, of equal importance, you will grow in self-confidence.

If, perchance, you run up against a wall and are unable to resolve the issue among yourselves, then make a note of it and ask your teacher.   Your group work will better prepare you to ask a clearer, more pin-pointed question for your teacher which, in turn, will make it easier for him to help you come to the right understanding.

Alternatively, you could also go online to find the answer. Just be sure that you find an authoritative source.   Look for sources that bear the name, for example, Longman, Oxford, Cambridge.

Our new view

I trust this book will provide you, as we have emphasized, with a new view to learning English, a view that will cause a change in your perception, and subsequently, your ease in learning English.

I do not claim to have all the answers.   No one does.   I feel, however, that I have provided you with a solid foundation, a new view that will serve you well while you are at home in China as well as when you are in an English-speaking country, a view on which you can build and grow.

Allow me to remind you that all the concepts discussed in this book are geared solely to your needs, i.e., the native speaker of Chinese learning English.   They will undoubtedly unlock the world of English for you, IF YOU GIVE THEM YOUR CAREFUL ATTENTION,

CONSIDERATION AND PRACTICE.   They highlight the pitfalls of the Chinese speaker learning English.   Concentrate on them and you're well on your way to mastering English.   I repeat: Put your attention on them and you'll be on the road to mastering English.

As we stated in the beginning, the concepts in this book are based on my firsthand experience teaching hundreds of Chinese students, observing them repeatedly—unwittingly—making the same mistakes in English, seeing that they did not have a grasp of what English really is.   My purpose has been to help you change your perspective, to pinpoint your mistakes and, by investigation, to help you correct them so that you can become competent speakers and writers of English.   Throughout, my standpoint stresses the importance of 1) becoming aware of your weaknesses, your mistakes and 2) gaining mastery by working on them and practicing them, and, as an essential by-product, 3) learning how to learn.

Your flat tire(s)

With this in mind, I would kindly ask that you consider the following.   If you had a flat tire in the front right wheel of your car, would you change the rear left wheel?   Of course not!   You'd put your attention where the problem is: the front right tire.   It's virtually

the same in mastering English.   Concentrate on the areas that need

your attention, all of which I have identified for you in the preceding

pages.   Always repair the tire(s) that will get you up and running, that

will get you to your destination!

It's in your hands

The points highlighted in this book will open doors to your

ongoing, ever-expanding understanding and mastery of English.   I

have no doubt that your English will improve by leaps and bounds, if

you follow the guidance that I have outlined for you herewith.

Learning, as we have pointed out, is about change.   Remember, no

change, no learning.   However, you are the only one who can initiate

and put into practice the change.   In other words, the change is in your

hands, in your mind.   Put another way, it's your decision.   I can show

you the areas that you need to work on, provide you with a new view,

but it, ultimately, depends on you!   You, then, are the one who has to

take responsibility for your learning.   You are the only one who can

do it!   PLEASE KEEP IN MIND THAT LEARNING TO THINK

FOR YOURSELF AND TRUSTING YOUR OWN INTUITION IS AS

IMPORTANT AS GRAMMAR, PUNCTUATION AND
VOCABULARY!   Practicing these important qualities in all your
investigations will translate into greater self-confidence and, thus,
success.

At the heart of it all

I trust that you are now fully aware that all the concepts in this
book require a change in your way of thinking.   That is to say, they
require that you open your mind to a different way of perceiving the
world around you.   You will never master English, dear student, if you
continue to think only in Chinese.   Please remember that learning a
second language, by it's very nature, requires A DIFFERENT
PATTERN OF THINKING.

When English, for example, says "**a** book," this reflects a
different pattern of thinking from your native Chinese.   When English
says "10 car**s**," this, again, reflects a different pattern of thinking from
your native Chinese.   When English says, "I wash**ed**," this reflects a
different pattern of thinking from your native Chinese.   Every English
concept in this book reflects A DIFFERENT PATTERN OF
THINKING from Chinese, from what you are used to.   This is AN

ESSENTIAL PRINCIPLE, an essential attitude that should always be present in all your investigations.   Please don't lose sight of this. Your progress, your success, your mastery of English depends upon it. Your responsibility, then, is to meet these challenges—this new view— and to integrate them into your understanding.   Trust me, YOU CAN DO IT!

* * * * *

We have now come to the end of our journey together.   In closing, I would like to thank you, dear student, for your careful, thoughtful consideration of the ideas that you have encountered in *What English Really is*.   It has been my pleasure to share my understanding with you.   I trust it will serve you well, that it will put you on the right path, that it will provide you a lifelong solid foundation on which to grow and expand, that it will open the door to the joy of learning—and using—English.

Allow me to leave you with the following insights.   It is my hope that their wisdom will be of as much value to you as they have been to me.

Education is not the learning of facts,

but the training of the mind to think.

—Albert Einstein (1879-1955)

Knowing is not enough; we must apply.

Willing is not enough; we must do.

—Johann Wolfgang von Goethe (1749-1832)

The true person learns without scholarship.

—Lao Tzu

What English Really Is: A Self-Study Guide for Chinese Students to Master English is also available in Chinese translation under the title:

被誤會的英語, 一本掌握英語的自學指南

About the Author

Ron Little has more than 40 years experience teaching ESL at the college level.   His students come from a wide variety of language backgrounds in Asia, the Middle East, Central and South America, Europe and Africa.

His extensive experience includes teaching in intensive ESL programs as well as tutoring writing to international students on a one-to-one basis in a university Writing Center environment.

He holds a B.A. and an M.A.T. degree. However, his study with Dr. Caleb Gattegno at Educational Solutions (NY, NY), over the course of several years, has had the greatest influence on his understanding of learning and teaching.

Author: Ron Little
Email: prof.ronlittle@gmail.com

Hal Richman
Email: halrichman@gmail.com

Cover calligraphy and layout by Ron Little
Email: ronlittleletters@gmail.com

Printed in Great Britain
by Amazon

79197003R00161